feeling fit

feeling fit

Aileen Ludington, M.D.

REVIEW AND HERALD® PUBLISHING ASSOCIATION
HAGERSTOWN, MD 21740

This book was
Edited by Jeannette R. Johnson
Copyedited by Jocelyn Fay and James Cavil
Designed by Patricia S. Wegh
Cover illustration by © Jennie Oppenheimer/SIS
Cartoons by Ellis R. Jones
Typeset: 11/12 Century Schoolbook

PRINTED IN U.S.A.

00 99 98 97   5 4 3 2 1

R&H Cataloging Service
Ludington, Aileen
    Feeling fit.

    1. Health.   2. Physical fitness.   3. Health self-care.   I. Title.

                        613

ISBN 0-8280-1284-9

Dedication

To the very special people who shared these very special stories, and to Dr. Clifford Ludington, my patient, long-suffering husband, who took over most of the household chores while I wrote this book.

Acknowledgments

The stories in this book are about people who made lifestyle and medication changes with the guidance of qualified health professionals. We urge you to do the same.

NOT TOO LATE

"My weight is the same as it was when I got married. I only regret I didn't start this lifestyle sooner—I feel years younger."—*Lincoln Steed, editor,* Listen *magazine*

BETTER SUCCESS

"I never had this kind of success treating these diseases in private practice."—*Ray Pellow, M.D.*

EXTRA YEARS

"What I learned at NEWSTART has added 14 years to my life."—*Father Fergus McGuiness*

FANTASTIC EXPERIENCE

"I shudder to think where I'd be today if I had not had my fantastic NEWSTART experience."—*H.M.S. Richards, speaker emeritus,* Voice of Prophecy *radio broadcast*

NO PAIN

"At 89, it's wonderful to get up in the morning and not hurt anywhere!"—*Mavis Lindgren, marathoner*

INCREDIBLY SIMPLE

"It's absolutely incredible that such basically simple lifestyle factors can initiate results like this in such a short time."—*Moses Yun, M.D.*

BETTER RELATIONSHIPS

"What I learned at NEWSTART seems to me to be in beautiful harmony with God's original plans for us. My spiritual life and relationship with Jesus are deeper and more real than I ever dreamed possible."—*Marie Anderson, cancer survivor*

LIVING PROOF

"I'm living proof that you can beat the odds of heart disease, even if it runs in your family."—*William Castelli, M.D.*

PHYSICIANS' ALERT

"Medical students, residents, and practicing physicians need an understanding of Lifestyle Medicine if they are going to treat today's killer diseases successfully."—*Vincent Gardner, M.D.*

Contents

Do Seventh-day Adventists Live Longer?

Epidemiological studies that have been going on since 1960 would indicate that those Adventists who pursue a certain lifestyle do indeed live longer.

The Adventist Mortality Study (begun in 1950) and the Adventist Health Study (begun in 1974)—with 25,000 and 34,000 California Adventists enrolled, respectively—are providing a wealth of information that is continuing to yield important findings. More than 150 articles published in peer review journals have attracted much attention in scientific circles and are widely quoted in literature.

Several unique characteristics of Adventists make them a most suitable population for epidemiological research. These include:

1. Sufficient variation in lifestyle.

2. Excellent cooperation in responding to research requests and filling out extensive questionnaires.

3. High degree of accuracy in reporting health habits.

During the past 30 years, more than $11 million has been set aside by the National Institutes for Health to fund extensive studies of Adventists at California's Loma Linda University.

Gary E. Fraser, M.D., Ph.D. (professor of epidemiology at Loma Linda University's School of Public Health), is the principal investigator for the Adventist Health Study and is the director for the Center for Health Research at LLU. "In the Adventist Health Study we are comparing *Adventists* with one lifestyle to *Adventists* who adhere to a different lifestyle," Fraser says. "The success of this study is in large part determined by the fact that Adventists do subscribe to a wide variety of dietary and exercise habits."

He reports that Adventists divided into groups according to their differing dietary patterns also have differing mortality patterns. He compared, for instance, Adventists who consume higher quantities of red meat, fatty foods, eggs, and coffee with those who emphasize more fruits, grains, beans, and vegetables, and also with those who consume smaller amounts of most foods (and, thus, probably consuming relatively few calories).

Interestingly, the high-fat/meat group had a risk of dying almost four times greater than either of the other two dietary patterns in the younger age groups (30 to 50 years). This advantage remained discernible and substantial in people up into the 80s. Frazer found that:

▶ being relatively thin confers an extra three to four years of life.

▶ eating a diet high in fruits, grains, beans, and vegetables confers an extra four to five years of life.

▶ a nonsmoking, relatively thin Adventist eating a diet high in fruit, grain, beans, and vegetables, and who exercises moderately may reasonably expect an extra 10 to 12 years of life as compared to a relatively overweight, nonexercising, high-fat/meat-consuming Adventist.

Fraser's group found that the higher consumption of fruits and beans and the lower consumption of animal flesh foods was especially associated with a lower risk for cancers of the lung, gastrointestinal tract, and urogenital systems. Other findings of interest include:

▶ For fatal coronary heart disease, men who consumed beef at least three times a week had a 60 to 70 percent increased risk. Similarly, women had about 30 percent increased risk.

▶ The data suggests that the consumption of whole-wheat bread was associated with a 40 percent decrease in risk of both fatal and nonfatal heart disease.

▶ Frequent consumption of nuts (at least four times a week) was associated with cutting the coronary risk in half, when compared to people who ate very few nuts.

▶ Smoking had a clearly defined association with risk of coronary heart disease and a substantial elevation of risk for leukemia and myeloma.

▶ Hypertension, physical inactivity, obesity, and diabetes mellitus were also significantly increased coronary risk.

SO WHAT ARE THOSE SECRETS TO A LONGER, HEALTHIER LIFE?

In this book NEWSTART is used as an acronym. Each letter represents one of the eight natural remedies: Nutrition (a return to a simpler, more natural diet); Exercise (daily, active); Water; Sunshine; Temperate, balanced lifestyle; Air (fresh); Rest; and Trust in God.*

These simple remedies are proving to be the most effective means available for preventing and/or treating today's epidemic of noninfectious diseases. Health promotion efforts and centers teaching NEWSTART principles are springing up around the world. The treatments are basically the same, and astounding results are obtained in an almost predictable fashion.

The term NEWSTART, as used in this book, represents Adventist health principles and lifestyle. (See Appendixes 1 and 2 for details.) NEWSTART, capitalized as one word, is the registered trademark adopted by Weimar Institute, in California, for its health conditioning center, NEWSTART Lifestyle Center. For the purposes of this book, we have obtained permission to use the term NEWSTART in a broader sense, that is, to also represent the many other devoted educators and centers that teach and live these principles. Much of my clinical experience has come from my work at Weimar Institute, as many of the stories in this book reflect. —*Aileen Ludington, M.D.*

---

*Ellen G. White, *The Ministry of Healing* (Mountain View, Calif.: Pacific Press Pub. Assn., 1905), pp. 234-286.

Foreword

C hurches need to be . . . less like untouchable cathedrals and more like well-used hospitals, places to bleed in rather than monuments to look at . . . places where you can take your mask off and let your hair down . . . places where you can have your wounds dressed," notes a recent *Adventist Review* article.[1]

Time magazine, in a cover story on faith and healing, reported that a growing number of people want to examine the connection between healing and spirituality. There is a yearning among patients for a more personal, more spiritual approach to their ills. There exists a growing disenchantment with modern, high-tech medicine that isn't working well with our common, chronic diseases.

The *Time* reporter then comments, "Not only do patients with chronic health problems fail to find relief in a doctor's office, but the endless high-tech scans and tests of modern medicine often leave them feeling alienated and uncared for. Many seek solace in the offices of alternative therapists and faith healers—to the tune of $30 billion a year, by some estimates."[2]

In the United States nearly 1 million deaths each year are caused by the progressive narrowing of people's arteries because of atherosclerotic plaques. That accounts for every second death! Americans suffer 1.5 million heart attacks annually. They also suffer 500,000 strokes. Some 60 million (35 percent of all adults) are afflicted with cardiovascular diseases. And yet this common disease, atherosclerosis, with its clinical manifestations—heart disease, strokes, angina, hypertension, claudication, impotence, certain forms of kidney disease and adult diabetes—*is largely caused by what we eat and how we live.*

The answer to these Western killer diseases is not found in more surgeries and more medications; they usually only relieve *symptoms.* The answer is to be found in attacking their causes. We need to change our lifestyle! And this involves understanding, education, and motivation.

In 1960 medical care consumed 5 percent of our nation's

income; it now consumes 15 percent. Many people can no longer afford medical care. Debilitating and deadly chronic diseases are at an all-time high. People everywhere are looking for ways to improve their health and to enjoy a longer, healthier life.

In 1988 C. Everett Koop, M.D., then surgeon general of the United States, issued a 712-page comprehensive report on nutrition and health. His main conclusion was that "the greatest challenge in medicine today is to be found in motivating people to assume responsibility for a health-affirming lifestyle."

Jesus provided the model on how to minister to people, reaching their "felt needs." One Christian author writes, "The Saviour mingled with men as one who desired their good. He showed His sympathy for them, ministered to their needs, and won their confidence. Then [and only then] He bade them, 'Follow Me.'"[3]

One way Jesus reached people (and the primary method by which He won their confidence) was by healing their illnesses. He wept with them. He comforted them. And He gave them hope. His touch is just as much needed today as it was then.

Through the stories of this book you will discover how burned-out, stressed-out, emotionally damaged, and chronically ill people are finding comfort and healing. The greatest need of the world right now just may be a simple yet profound ministry: doing what Jesus did—sharing, educating, inspiring, loving people.

This is the message I find in this book. This is the dream I share with the author, who is my friend.

—*Hans A. Diehl, Dr.H.Sc., M.P.H., C.N.S.*

---

[1] Charles Swindoll, *Dropping Your Guard* (Word Books, 1983), p. 127, in Randy Maxwell, "A Place to Bleed," *Adventist Review,* Apr. 18, 1996.

[2] *Time,* June 24, 1996.

[3] E. G. White, *The Ministry of Healing,* p. 143.

Introduction

This is a book of stories about real people battling real diseases who turned to Adventist health principles for relief and healing. They are true experiences of persons Dr. Hans Diehl or I have interviewed or known personally, some for many years. You will feel their pain and experience their hope as they grapple with difficult health problems, sometimes fighting for their very lives.

This book deals with what people can do for themselves against the so-called Western diseases that are reaching near-epidemic levels in developed parts of the world. They are increasingly being referred to as "lifestyle" diseases, because most of them relate to the way people eat and live.

I grew up believing in Ellen G. White's counsel on health matters and benefiting from the Adventist lifestyle. But there seemed no place in the modern medical world for such simple, largely unspectacular treatments this nineteenth-century author recommended. Further, since much of what she taught conflicted with scientific findings of that time, Seventh-day Adventist hospitals and doctors faced the challenge of protecting their credibility.

But all that has changed. The principal diseases maiming and killing people today are diseases for which the medical profession has little to offer besides palliation, powerful drugs, and symptomatic measures. There are no miracle drugs for curing diabetes and no quick fixes to restore diseased heart arteries to wholeness. Dr. Lawrence Power got to the heart of the problem in one of his syndicated health columns. "Health is an inside job," he wrote. "Most of today's disabilities are self-inflicted wounds that are proving quite resistant to high-cost technology. We've got to change our ways."

And incredibly, the latest scientific findings for "changing our ways" confirm the very simple, natural remedies the Bible and Ellen White laid out so long ago.

Many of the stories in this book are about people who found help by joining live-in programs. The advantage of "living in" is that maximum results can be realized in minimum time. Other stories come from doctors' offices, health seminars, weight control groups, personal counseling, and from overseas sources. A number of stories are about people who worked out their own NEWSTART programs.

My purpose in recording these stories is to help you better understand how—and why—the things we eat and the way we live impact the kinds of diseases we get, many of which are stumping medical science today.

Do you not know?

Have you not heard?

The Lord is the everlasting God,

the Creator of the ends of the earth.

He will not grow tired or weary,

and his understanding no one can fathom.

He gives strength to the weary

and increases the power of the weak.

Even youths grow tired and weary,

and young men stumble and fall;

but those who hope in the Lord

will renew their strength.

They will soar on wings like eagles;

they will run and not grow weary,

they will walk and not be faint.

—Isaiah 40:28-31, NIV

Lifestyle and Obesity:

Meet the Fun People!

Those who know tell us that on the average Americans are heavier than the citizens of any other major nation. My corollary is that the heaviest ones among us also carry a most endearing sense of humor. Their problems may be weighty, but they can always find the lighter side. . . .

Valentine chocolates are always one of the great mysteries of life. . . . How can one pound, in the shape of a heart, add two pounds to the shape of your bottom?

The Dieters Prayer: Lord, lead me not into temptation—I can find it easily enough on my own.

Self-control: A caramel may go undevoured, but not undesired.

Dieting tip: Pieces of cookies contain no calories. The process of breaking causes calorie leakage.

There used to be days when I climbed on and off the scales so many times that it almost qualified as a step-aerobics class. —Jeni LaBelle

There's also the wistful side:

. . . to slide into a booth at a restaurant.

. . . to sit in a tourist seat and fly to Hawaii.

. . . to buy clothes from the racks again, instead of sending for "fat" sizes.

. . . to get out of a chair without using my hands.

. . . to be able to just sit down and not worry about breaking the chair.

And the bad news side:

• *Extra weight shortens life. (Even 10 pounds increases mortality figures.)*

• *Excess weight lays the foundation for every degenerative (lifestyle) disease except osteoporosis. For example, obese people are three times more likely to have heart disease, four times more likely to suffer from high blood pressure, five times more likely to develop diabetes and elevated blood cholesterols, and six times more likely to have gallbladder disease.*

● *Overweight people develop more cancers of the colon, breast, prostate, cervix, rectum, uterus and ovaries; and they suffer more osteoarthritis and back pain.*

● *Extra weight affects self-image, adding a heavy psychological burden.*

But the good news is the rewards of losing excess weight are enormous. However, for many people, remaining overweight would be less harmful than endlessly playing the rhythm game of girth control. So unless you are in dead earnest, stay out of the game.

Throughout this book you will read story after story of the near-miraculous results that success brings. Next to quitting smoking, attaining and maintaining an ideal weight is the greatest favor you can do for your health.

Now for some real-life stories of real-life people waging real-life battles. . . .

STORY 1:

The Couch Potato Fights Back

Nothing makes your sense of humor disappear faster than having somebody ask you where it is.—Avian Bell.

Something was wrong. I felt it the moment I stepped into the office. I offered my cheeriest smile, but the woman's eyes were cold and belligerent. Her husband was carefully studying the carpet. I seated myself and picked up her chart, hoping for a clue to her hostility. *Back pain. Thirteen years.* My head started to ache. Chronic back pain—one of the most difficult and discouraging problems doctors face. Only that morning I had told our medical director, "I'll take any kind of patient you want me to see today—except orthopedic cases, especially back problems. I just don't have enough background in that field." And after that little speech, I stepped into my office and met Lorine.

24

Meet the Fun People!

I took a deep breath and looked up, my eyes meeting hers. I smiled again and spoke as gently as I could. "I want to help you," I said. "Where would you like to begin?"

But she had been pushed too far—the dam broke. "I don't want to be here!" She spit the words out bitterly. "I've been forced to come. My own family did this to me, and I'm angry—*furious!*" Her eyes burned like hot coals. "This is the most humiliating thing that's ever happened to me. I'm a mature adult, and I'm being treated like a 5-year-old child." Her voice, tight with emotion, wilted into a sob.

I jumped up. "I'm sorry," I heard myself saying. "There must be some mistake. We don't keep people here against their will. Come, I'll help you arrange to go home."

She obviously hadn't expected this. She glanced at her husband. He shifted uncomfortably and continued to stare at the floor, stricken. Finally he looked up. "I— We— We did it because we want to help her," he said. "We didn't know she'd be so upset."

Lorine leaned back in her chair, her anger subsiding. She changed tactics. "Doctor, it would just be a waste of your time." Her voice was matter-of-fact now. "I've seen 11 doctors and had at least 100 X-rays. They say surgery won't help. And I've tried everything else."

I sensed despair behind her words. She was a chronic case. She'd worn out her doctors as well as her loved ones. She must insulate herself from further disappointment. I took her hands in mine. "Lorine, I know you can get better. You don't want to go on like this! Look, you're already here, and your care is paid for. How about giving the program a chance?"

Thank God, the words were right. The idea appealed to her. Lorine was basically a fighter, and she'd been handed a ray of hope. Her gaze became distant as she weighed the idea. "Why not?" she said finally. "I'm a sinking ship anyway." A moment later she straightened up. "But my family is not forgiven." Her eyes narrowed as she looked at her husband, but the anger and bitterness were gone.

Then Lorine poured out her story. "I was once a vital, energetic woman—deeply in love with life. Besides being a wife to my minister-husband and mother to five children, I had my own business and was actively involved with my church.

"Thirteen years ago I fell down a stairway and injured my back. I was bedfast for some time, and my recovery was slow and incomplete. The past 13 years have been a blur of struggle

25

and pain—always pain. My doctor told me surgery wouldn't help, but as the years went by I desperately looked for other, and better, specialists. I've had dozens of X-rays, but the answer is always the same: There is no operation that will help your problem. My active life disintegrated, and I spent more and more time in bed or on the couch.

"Five years ago a severe knee injury made matters worse. My life became a round of sleeping, watching television, eating, and getting fat. I became a world-class couch potato," she concluded with a little laugh.

She was spunkier than I thought.

But she wasn't finished. She shifted in her chair, lips quivering, fighting a sudden rush of emotion. "I just . . . feel . . . so helpless . . . so hopeless . . . such a terrible drag on my family." The tears flowed. "I'd be better off dead."

I put my arms around her and hugged her. "Lorine, Lorine, you are not dead! You are here for a reason. You must start getting well."

I walked with her to her next appointment. Kind, gentle people guided her through the rest of her tests and evaluations that day. She returned to her room, quiet and subdued.

> I know what it's like to be depressed. I know what it's like to plan one's suicide. The Lord gave me victory, and I know He can do it for you!

The next day she shared this experience with me. "Last night I decided to seal the commitment I've made. 'Dear God,' I prayed, 'I'm a total failure. No one knows better than You how many times I've failed, how many tears of disappointment I've shed. Tonight I pray for Your strength, Your blessing, Your power. I give You my will, totally surrendered.'"

Her fight was over. So were the anger, the bitterness, the resentment, and the hopelessness. Having made up her mind, Lorine began focusing on the task at hand. She attended everything. She soaked up the scientific sessions and didn't miss a cooking class. She asked questions and borrowed books. She befriended everyone she met. Instead of getting more X-rays, Lorine went outdoors to walk. Actually, walk is an exaggeration. She waddled, slowly and painfully. She carried 65 excess pounds on her five-foot-one-inch frame. At first she could go only around the flagpole, grasping her husband's arm. But she did it, again and again. Gradually her muscles strengthened and the walks lengthened. By the end of three weeks she was covering three to four miles a day.

There were no miracle drugs for Lorine, only an occasional pain reliever to dull her back pain. Food became her medicine. She ate three regular meals a day with nothing between except generous drinks of water. Her diet consisted of a variety of plant foods—fruits, vegetables, grains, and a few nuts, unprocessed and unrefined. Being a vegetarian, she did not miss the animal foods. Her caloric intake was trimmed to low but safe limits, and her diet was balanced so that she didn't feel hungry.

Within a few days Lorine's sense of humor revived, and her laughter rang out on the trails and in the dining hall. She organized a singing group and wrote poems. She reached out to her fellow patients. She wrote loving letters to her children.

The following week Lorine literally bounced into my office. "This program really works! I feel good already! In fact, I haven't been this energetic in years!" She paused, serious now, searching for the right words. "You know, this program isn't really that hard. Everything I'm doing here, I could do at home." Then she giggled. "Except for hydrotherapy (water treatments). I really love it when they put those hot packs on my back, then finish off with a good massage."

I explained to Lorine that to get well she must lose her excess weight. "Once you've normalized your weight, most of your other problems will take care of themselves," I assured her.

She made a graph on which she could chart her weekly weight, to help keep her motivated and to make sure her weight loss was gradual—between one and two pounds a week. At the end of her 25 days at the center Lorine was ecstatic. "I've lost nine and a half pounds, and my blood pressure is down from 170/114 to 130/80," she told anyone who would listen. Her blood cholesterol had dropped from 266 milligrams per deciliter (mg percent) to a much safer 194, and a threatening diabetic condition had disappeared.

To celebrate her last night with us, Lorine wrote and produced a very funny play, with her fellow patients acting the different parts. As we laughed and applauded, Lorine stepped to the microphone and raised her right hand. "Tonight, before this assembled throng, I solemnly swear to return one year from now—*in a size 10 dress!"* With her ample body still encased in her big tent dress, it was hard to imagine such a transformation—until I remembered how far she had come already.

Lorine did indeed "take the program home." A year later she dropped by for the promised visit—in a size 10 dress and with flowers in her hair. We could hardly recognize her. She was absolutely beautiful!

This is what she told us: "When I got home, I walked one hour every day and lived exactly as I lived here, and so did Peter." She glanced at her trim husband, who was watching her with love and pride. "Within a year I'd lost 60 pounds. My back pain completely disappeared, as did my knee pain. I resumed caring for my home and family. I read, studied, and honed my skills until I was ready to begin teaching cooking schools and nutrition classes at our church. Next, I started conducting weight-control programs. People identified with me, and God has blessed my efforts.

"I'm so glad I started fighting the right battles. Peter and I are still faithful to what we have learned, and I thank God for opening my eyes to ways in which I could cooperate in bringing about my own healing."

FIVE YEARS LATER: LORINE'S OWN STORY
No, I did not want to go to NEWSTART. I was tricked into it by my family, and I was furious. But I know now that a severely depressed person cannot make rational decisions. My family saved my life. I thank God for giving them the strength to stand up to me.

Weight was the last thing I wanted to think about that day, but I decided to stay. (I found out later that weight control was Dr. Ludington's special interest.) Staying with the program was a good idea. But I knew the "proof" would depend entirely on what I did when I got home.

I decided to stick with it. When I make a decision, I'm like a bulldog. During the 10 months it took to get the weight off, I became an absolute fanatic. A pastor and his wife are invited to many functions, most of which include eating in the late evening. At first I would say, "No, thank you. Could I have a glass of water?" Later I began carrying tea bags in my purse, and I'd say, "Oh, I'd be delighted if you would give me a cup of hot water so I can make some herb tea." I tried hard not to make people feel bad. I would always say, "It's what works for me."

Meet the Fun People!

After a while people stopped offering me junk and would have a cup of tea ready for me. Then we would both feel OK.

Since I reached my weight goal, I've been careful, but not fanatical. I walk one hour a day (which for me is about three miles), do calisthenics, take sunbaths, and drink about three quarts of water. I eat three wholesome meals five hours apart, and not one swallow (except water) between meals. I do this every day, with few exceptions. I weigh myself only once a week.

Before, I couldn't even sit up in the car. Now I rarely have any back pain. I have gradually lost an additional 10 pounds. It was an absolute miracle that I lost all that weight. Some people think miracles are instantaneous. But not necessarily. I followed all eight of God's health remedies to get well. That's why I'm wearing a size 10 dress today. I still keep one ugly size 22 dress in my closet just to keep me motivated.

You can see now why I'm thankful for Dr. Ludington. God knew I didn't need an orthopedic doctor for my back—I needed a weight doctor! After I lost the weight, my backaches and knee pain disappeared. So did my diabetes and hypertension. And so did my depression.

A few years ago I discovered I had multiple sclerosis. But I really believe that because I've followed God's plan for the past five years, I'm not nearly as disabled as other people I know who are around my age.

During the first year, while I was concentrating on getting well, the Lord gave me the idea of putting together a cookbook. I wrote the first edition to give me something to think about besides myself. But when I finished it, we had no money to publish it. Then God worked another miracle. My dad isn't well, but he was so proud of me and of what I was doing that he put a check in the mail, and we published the first edition. It is now in its third edition.

I must tell you about my third miracle. After I lost all my weight, I had to wear a girdle to look nice, and I hated that. I was advised to have that baggy apron of skin and fat removed by a plastic surgeon, but there was no way we could afford that, and insurance didn't pay for cosmetic procedures. I had a hernia that needed repair. Once my doctor understood my larger problem, he arranged for a plastic surgeon friend to operate with him and fix up my stomach, too. The plastic surgeon didn't charge me a penny, and my insurance covered all the rest.

Later I asked the plastic surgeon, "Why did you do this, when you knew we couldn't pay you?"

"Listen," he said, "I have lots of patients who pay me well. But once in a while, for my soul's sake, I like to do something for someone who really needs it."

Don't tell me the Lord doesn't care about the details of our lives!

Since I've been well I've conducted many seminars on nutrition, stress, and weight control. I do many cooking schools. I'm especially good at weight-control classes, because the people know I've been there. I know what it's like to hide food—and to eat at night, when your family is asleep. And to eat all day, when your family is at work or school. When people would come to the door selling cookies and candy, we never bought any— when my husband was home. If it was a good cause, we gave them money. But if I was home alone, I would buy four or five of everything and hide it in my dresser drawers.

I also know what it's like to be depressed. I know what it's like to plan one's suicide, because I did it on more than one occasion. But I also know the Lord can give victory. He did it for me, and I know He can do it for you!

STORY 2:

The Soda Pop Girl

"If you want to know if your brain is flabby, feel your legs."
—Bruce Barton.

Ruby Lee (not her real name) was beautiful. She was also the best operating room nurse I've ever known. I was an anesthesiologist in those days, and we worked together over a span of 15 years. I first met Ruby when she was 21, about three months after she'd graduated from nursing school in Bangkok, Thailand. I was a new missionary doctor who had just joined the staff. I was immediately attracted to this bright, friendly, energetic woman, and we became good friends.

I quickly learned a few things about my new home. Every day was humid. The seasons consisted of the hot season, the hotter season, and the rainy and dry seasons. During the rains the humidity became even worse. The city water was unsafe to drink. At home we boiled our water, cooled it, and stored it in jars in the refrigerator. Away from home we drank soda.

In those early days there was no air-conditioning in the operating room. Later, when it was installed, the electricity would frequently go off for indefinite periods. The machines themselves broke down fairly regularly. About midmorning every operating day, Ruby Lee brought in bottles of ice-cold soda. She would lift the face mask of each perspiring surgeon and nurse and hold the bottle as he/she gratefully gulped down the cool liquid through a straw. Each morning our operating room refrigerator was stocked with bottles of orange-flavored soda to which the operating room personnel had unlimited access. Those drinks became a survival tool.

During the next few years Ruby married and had children. Her trim, petite figure broadened and thickened. Her face began to puff. I often thought of the earlier days and felt saddened by what I saw happening to her body.

About that time I started a weight-control class for hospital workers. I was pleased that Ruby chose to join. As the weeks went by, most of the class struggled hard to lose a pound here and there. Some became discouraged and quit. But Ruby was different. Week after week her weight went down, down, down. When asked for the secret of her success, she would give only a bemused smile. I watched with delight as the attractive, shapely girl I had once known emerged once more.

On the last day I asked various class members to share the particular part of the program that had been most helpful to them. As we worked our way around the circle, it became Ruby's turn. She again smiled her bemused smile, and I held my breath. But this time she was ready to talk.

"I actually made only two changes in my lifestyle," she said. "I joined a gym and exercised for one hour every day after work— and I stopped drinking soda. I've lost 40 pounds and am back to my nursing school weight. I feel better than I have for years."

Ruby maintained her schoolgirl weight for at least the next 15 years, at which time I lost track of her.

A few fortunate people, such as Ruby, can identify the specific problem that is triggering their weight gain. Unfortunately, most of us need more comprehensive lifestyle changes.

STORY 3:

The Worm and the Butterfly
by Hans Diehl

Man is here for the sake of other men.—Albert Einstein.

My shirt stuck to my body like glue. I had been lecturing for nearly two hours to an audience of some 500 people in a sweltering camp meeting tent on a hot Wisconsin summer day. Another lecture was scheduled right after lunch. For once, I didn't want to see anyone or shake any hands. Nothing else was on my mind but to reach my air-conditioned room, where I could shower, rest, and reorganize my thoughts.

"Dr. Diehl, may I talk to you?" asked a timid voice at my elbow.

Oh, no, not now! my body screamed. But I stopped and turned to her. She was fortyish and definitely overweight. I had just finished my lecture entitled "How to Eat More and Weigh Less." I could see she wanted further counsel. My inner struggle continued. Surely her questions could wait. I had so many important things to do! But then I thought about my reason for being in this place—to help people sense God's love more effectively through better health.

"Please?" Her eyes were sad but hopeful.

We walked to an air-conditioned trailer that served as the sound studio for the convention. During the next two hours the stress and fatigue drained out of me, and my clothes gradually dried. I felt drawn to this struggling fellow pilgrim as I listened to Grace's pain as she talked about her home life. Her husband was a good provider, but a poor communicator. He said he loved her, but didn't live it. He led out in the life of the church, but hadn't prayed with her for years. With romance gone and intimacy a fading memory, they shared the same roof, but increasingly lived separate lives. She felt like a married single.

Depression soon followed. She felt worthless, lonely, unloved, used, and intimidated. Food became a pacifier, an outlet for her pain. She couldn't remember when her husband had last complimented her cooking or smiled when she dressed up for him. He was charming with strangers, but withdrawn at home. To make matters worse, the food added pounds, and her thickening figure deepened her discouragement.

Meet the Fun People!

I groped for the right words. What could I say? I naively suggested new lingerie or a different perfume. But even as I said those things, I knew better. She needed some Christian assertiveness training. But more than that, she needed emotional support, a feeling of worth. A Christian psychologist was not available, and the church "would not understand."

How inadequate I felt! I gave her a copy of my book *To Your Health* and inscribed the words: *Don't ever give up. The best is yet to come.* We prayed together, and I entrusted her to the care of the Good Shepherd. She left with tears in her eyes.

I wondered what had been accomplished. I had mainly just listened. But my clothes were dry now, and I felt relaxed. My pressured mind was decompressed. It was time for my next lecture.

Four months passed since that sweltering summer day. Then I received her letter.

Many, many thanks for coming to Wisconsin. Your good counsel, both in the seminar and in private, has changed my life. Not knowing where else to start, I began with the diet. I followed all of it to the letter. I have lost 22 pounds and am still going down. I walk as regularly as possible. I've also lost most of my aches and pains. My feet, ankles, and eyes no longer get puffy, and my blood pressure is coming down. I feel great! My friends tell me I have a special glow. To my surprise, after one week my husband joined me in this new way of eating. He has lost 23 pounds and feels better than he has for years.

Your personal counsel has been important too. Soon after I got home, my husband and I came very close to breaking up. I just felt like the blackboard of my life was filled up with pain and sorrow, and there wasn't room left to write any more grief on it. Nothing had ever been resolved.

When it finally came down to the line, my husband agreed to sit down and talk. At long last we really communicated. The result was simply that we forgave each other for everything and started over fresh. He is such a different man now, and I realize I am a different woman. He still does all the aggravating things he ever did (can a leopard change his spots?), but they no longer bother me, because he is learning to make me feel loved. He urges me to stay with the dietary program. He calls me "skinny," and I love it. He makes an effort to be attentive and romantic. And I'm doing a bigger share of loving too. Gladly! (New nightgowns and all!)

How prophetic you were when you wrote in your book, "The best is yet to come." Since we forgave and started over, life has be-

come sweet as honey. It's as though the years of pain and anguish had never happened. My joy is so great that yesterday I got down on my knees and sang the doxology! And it felt perfectly right.

I sat for a long time holding the letter, recalling that day. It seemed I had done so little. Yet God had blessed the intent of my heart and fused it with her need. He had used me—tired, sweaty, reluctant, in the worst circumstances—to extend His healing touch to another. And now I too felt like singing the doxology. The promise jumped to my mind: "Cast your bread upon the waters, for you will find it after many days" (Eccl. 11:1, RSV).

In this case, it came back buttered.

FOUR YEARS LATER: GRACE'S OWN STORY

The worm writhed inside its cocoon. It had been there so long. There seemed no way out. The doors and windows had been sealed shut. I was that worm. I could scarcely remember what it felt like to be free and in control of my life. For 30 years I had been increasingly hemmed in by external and internal habits. So many things had gone wrong.

I thought as I struggled, *Why do I feel so trapped? Why can't I break out of this cocoon? Where is God? Am I to go to my death without realizing any meaning to my life?*

Somewhere in the dim past I had married and borne two wonderful children. But from the beginning the marriage was very stressful. I didn't know how to cope, how to turn negative experiences into positive growth. When I felt down, I'd make my usual circle in the kitchen, beginning at the refrigerator, proceeding to the cupboard, moving to the freezer, then back to the refrigerator. As the years rolled on, so did the pounds. Then came the merry-go-round of dieting—10 pounds down, then 15 pounds back up. I couldn't keep it off. Year after year I struggled through the demoralizing routine of losing a little weight, then gaining back more. My self-esteem plummeted.

"I want out! I want out!" I cried over and over, but I couldn't find a way. I had bound myself securely inside a cocoon of a bad lifestyle and depression. Death seemed the only solution, but the thought terrified me.

Finally my struggles ceased. I was worn out, tired of failure, tired of hating myself. In desperation I cried out, "Lord, if You don't do something for me, I'm not going to make it!" Bitter tears flooded my cheeks as I gave up the fight.

Two weeks later I went to camp meeting. I don't know why

34

I ended up going, but I like to think the Lord gave me the necessary shove. The health speaker that week was a Dr. Hans Diehl, a heart disease researcher from Loma Linda, California. He quoted scientific data suggesting that most Western killer diseases, such as atherosclerosis, adult diabetes, high blood pressure, and strokes, could be avoided, even reversed.

When he mentioned strokes, he had my complete attention. My mother, father, and their parents had all died of strokes. I figured that's what I had to look forward to.

Dr. Diehl talked about eating more and weighing less by markedly reducing the intake of fats, oils, sugars, cholesterol, and salt, and by eating more wholesome grain products, beans, potatoes, fruits, and vegetables. He spoke with authority, showing us step by step how we could avoid the very things we dreaded.

I sought out the young doctor and blurted out my story, one he'd probably heard a hundred times before. He encouraged me and autographed my book "Don't ever give up. The best is yet to come."

> **My attitude about God got straightened out. I now realize He was with me all the time, waiting for me to give Him permission to work in my life.**

God only knows how badly I wanted to believe that. A spark of hope appeared. Maybe I could become the woman I once had been. Maybe I could avoid the disease that had prematurely claimed my parents and grandparents. Maybe my marriage wasn't hopeless.

As I returned to my room, my spark of hope burst into a blaze. My self-esteem returned. My new lifestyle began with my very next meal. And the next morning I joined the exercise class.

There followed a year of intense and dynamic change for me, a metamorphosis from an old, overweight, tired, listless "worm" into an energetic, slimmer, healthier, happier "butterfly." It was a year that brought me closer to God and to a new understanding of how to incorporate His health principles into my daily life.

With new hope, I began to dream again. With a new attitude I began to set goals. Most important, my attitude about God got straightened out. I now realize He was with me all the time, but was just waiting for me to give Him permission to work in my life. From this heart knowledge came the sweet return of my self-worth, and from that, the healing of our marriage. Praise God, my husband and I have been on a beautiful honeymoon ever since!

Physically, I'm getting younger instead of older. My aches and pains have disappeared. Forty pounds have melted away, and I'm still losing. My blood pressure is down to 120/70, and my cholesterol is 139 mg/% (3.6 mmol/l). I walk regularly and have as much energy and endurance as I had at age 21.

As I emerged from my cocoon, people noticed the "new me" and began asking questions. What a splendid opportunity to share with them what I'd learned. Then they began asking for recipes and practical guidelines. As a result, I printed a recipe book aptly entitled, "Getting Started on the Optimal Diet." I'm frequently called on to do public speaking, telling my story to church and civic groups. I do lots of counseling, and I took a writing course at a local college. I have since become a published writer.

Now, on the fourth anniversary of my "cocoon breakout," I thank God again for all He has done for me. At times I have to pinch myself to believe that I'm the same woman who, only four years ago, was depressed, lonely, and suicidal. Yet it is I, but with a whole new mind-set, new energy, and a drive to help others.

I'm eager to share my experience with anyone who is tempted to feel too old, too tired, too hopeless to go on fighting. Begin with your health. As that improves, other good things will start coming.

Yes, Dr. Diehl, four years ago you wrote, "The best is yet to come." You were right! For me, the best did come. By putting into daily practice God's principles for healthful living, this worm has become a butterfly. Praise God!

STORY 4:

My Closest Friends Were My Dogs
by Arnold Cox (name supplied)

I mean it! My closest friends were my dogs, because they did not insult me. I'm 42 years old, and a few months ago I weighed 290 pounds. I avoided people, because they either pitied me or preached at me. I guess I was pitiable, because I could not walk even a half block without severe leg pain. My knees and feet hurt so badly that my physician wanted to put me on a disability pension. But I wasn't ready to give up on life yet. Actually, I am a Seventh-day Adventist, but like so many of us boomers I paid little attention to Adventist health principles while growing up. It took a lot of suffering to finally wake me up.

When I heard about a health lecture entitled "Eat More and Weigh Less," I thought, *Just what I need.* The week before I had managed to go without doughnuts for a whole week—then felt so deprived I ate a dozen at one sitting. Yes, I definitely needed help.

I ended up attending the entire four-week Coronary Health Improvement Project (CHIP) being held in our community. At this citywide community health seminar, conducted by Dr. Hans Diehl, I bought a book and some cassette tapes and followed the instructions carefully at home. It felt good to start caring for my body in God's way.

It's been six months now, and I have dropped 100 pounds. I am aiming to lose another 30 pounds slowly to reach my normal weight. With this new way of eating I don't feel hungry at all. The program cost me a lot—I've had to buy all new clothes! But I'm not complaining. My breathing is normal, I can see my feet, I walk six miles a day without pain, my migraines have disappeared, and I work full-time.

No, I'm not complaining. Every way I look at it, I got a real bargain.

STORY 5:

I Lost 1,405 Pounds

I've lost 1,405 pounds, and I'm still fat," Elizabeth announced as she seated herself. "The year 1961 was a disaster for me. That was when I changed from an attractive, shapely woman into a fat blob."

The woman I was looking at was attractive, carefully groomed, and tastefully dressed. Overweight, yes, but certainly no "fat blob." I started to object, but she wasn't finished.

"That year I was pregnant, gained too much weight, had my

baby, and didn't lose a single pound. Shocked and frantic, I launched into a crash diet that solved the problem. Briefly. The next 19 years became a nightmarish search for a way to become a normal human being again. I tried just about every diet that's been invented. I've spent years taking pills and expensive shots. I've joined spas, been wrapped, massaged, and belted. I've tried acupuncture, hypnosis, and aversion therapy. I've flown to foreign countries for promising experimental treatments. During those 19 years I lost a total of 1,405 pounds and spent at least $25,000. But I'm just as fat today as I was in 1961."

This woman was incredible—so open, so honest, so direct—and yet so absolutely frantic.

"About a year ago I spent nearly a month at the Pritikin Longevity Center," she continued. "I was thrilled with what I learned. Their emphasis on healthful living made sense to me. No fads, no gimmicks, no shots or medicine. Gradually I parted with many of my bad habits—coffee, tea, colas, and alcohol, as well as my high-sugar, high-fat, refined-food diet. I lost 14 pounds there, and another 20 as I continued the program at home."

"That sounds much like our program here," I said. "What happened?"

"I am a businesswoman, the head of a large real estate company. After a few weeks I found myself unable to maintain the heavy exercise program required. Also, the seven or eight small meals I was supposed to eat each day did not fit into my busy, pressured life. As the stresses and pains built up, my willpower gradually vanished into a flood of indulgences.

"One day I woke up and realized I'd put 20 pounds back on. And after all I'd been through! I felt discouraged, depressed, and desperate. I couldn't leave my work just then to return to Pritikin, so I joined a local weight-control program. They got me back on an exercise schedule and gave me a diet supplement program. This entailed taking lots of vitamins, minerals, enzymes, hormones, and other nutritional supplements. It added up to 72 pills to swallow each day and cost $200 per month. These were supposed to supply me with energy and decrease my desire for food. I conscientiously adhered to this program for 13 weeks—and gained 13 pounds! Well, that did it. I went a little berserk. My life was out of control, my nights were full of nightmares—dreams of being choked, drowned, trapped somewhere, overwhelmed. I became fearful and withdrawn.

"About then I saw a short segment on the evening news

about your health center. I saw people hiking on beautiful mountain trails and thought *This place sounds as good as the longevity center—and it's less expensive and closer.* My husband told me it was a Christian place and that I'd be uncomfortable with that. 'Besides,' he added, 'you'd be bored without TV.' Still, I found myself wanting to come. So here I am." She looked at me expectantly.

"You say you aren't a Christian," I began carefully. "But somehow I feel that God sent you here. You need so much more than just another diet and exercise program."

She leaned toward me. "What do you want me to do?"

I explained the basics of our program and urged her to involve herself in everything. "I hope you'll come to our morning devotionals," I added. "And do make friends with members of our staff."

"I'll come to everything, so don't worry. Despite my husband's opinion, I have no fear of Christians," she said, laughing. "But what about all these pills?"

"Why don't you cut down to 50 a day," I suggested, testing her attachment to them.

Two days later she told me, "I couldn't face those pills any longer. I dumped them in the trash." She knew she didn't need them and felt good about making her own decision.

At her next appointment Elizabeth was more relaxed. Her voice had lost its frantic edge. "This place is so peaceful," she observed. "Everyone is so kind, so warm and happy, that it's hard for me to believe a place like this really exists. . . . Oh, and the devotionals—I love them! Those sweet nurses and students play their guitars and sing with us. I've learned several scripture songs already. And the hydrotherapy treatments are delightful! I was treated with so much love and care that I was much moved. At the end of my treatment the young woman offered a short prayer for my health and healing. I felt like weeping." Her voice softened. "How could this gentle, beautiful young woman care so much for a big, fat, middle-aged slob?"

Uh-oh, putting herself down again. But she did it with such good humor I knew her obsession with herself was weakening. She was beginning to reach out to others. During the next few days Elizabeth absorbed the spiritual atmosphere like a thirsty sponge. She asked questions and began reading her Bible. By the third week she was ready to talk.

"When I came here, I was totally unhappy and miserable in

my personal life, yet I had not felt any need for spiritual things. In fact, I was in the middle of a determined four-year effort to accumulate a maximum of material possessions. I filled my home with antiques and imported furniture. I bought expensive jewelry. I drove the finest Cadillac. But none of these things helped. I was still miserable and empty inside.

"But during my time here I've realized that you people have something I want. My nightmares have stopped, and my fears are fading. I'm beginning to feel an inner peace." She paused and looked out the window, seeming to search for just the right words. When she looked back, her eyes were large and serious. "I want to give my heart to Jesus," she said simply.

I felt God's presence in the room. We knelt together, and I prayed for her. Then, in a halting voice, she began to pray. "Lord . . . I've never . . . prayed before. I'm not sure how to do it. But I want to give my heart to You, to be a Christian."

We hugged each other and walked back to the lodge together.

The next day she brought her Bible to my office. "Look!" she said with excitement. "The Lord gave me a special text, just for me, just what I need." She pointed to Isaiah 41:13 and read, "'I am the Lord, your God, who takes hold of your right hand and says to you, Do not fear; I will help you' [NIV]. Since I've given my heart to the Lord, I've found an inner calm and security I never want to lose. I feel a happiness and satisfaction I haven't known in years.

"I came here to lose weight," she went on, "but I am going home with infinitely more. Yes, I've learned how to lose weight. But my deepest gratitude is for the change within. The spiritual one. The peaceful, joyful heart.

"I'm not a loser anymore," Elizabeth said with conviction. "With God holding my right hand, I am a winner."

STORY 6:

Too Fat for the Job

applied for this job I really wanted," Wanee told me. "I qualified in every way except for my appearance. 'Too fat,' they said.

"My father discovered MHPC [Mission Health Promotion

Meet the Fun People!

Center, a branch of Bangkok Adventist Hospital in Thailand] and enrolled me in a NEWSTART program. He told me he didn't want to see my face until I reached a more normal weight. I weighed 236 pounds at that time."

An intelligent, highly educated young woman, Wanee came from an affluent Thai family. To my delight, she spoke English well enough to dispense with a translator. Here is the way she described her first two weeks:

"There were three things I strongly disliked before coming to MHPC—exercise, beans, and vegetables. And yes, you guessed it, those three things made up my life in this place!

"On the second day I tried to hike up a small hill, but I couldn't make it all the way to the top. In fact, I could barely make it back to the center. And I'm only 28 years old.

"I love to swim," she continued, "so I swam the length of the pool as fast as I could. I had no strength to swim back. I could see that my fitness level was very low.

"I kept walking and swimming every day. At the end of the two weeks I was walking seven miles in the morning and swimming two rounds [twice the length of the pool] each afternoon."

Wanee stayed at our center for 77 days and lost 46 pounds. By the last month she was walking seven to 10 miles and swimming 40 rounds per day.

"I didn't ever feel hungry," she said of the experience, "even though I ate less than half as much as I had been eating before. I felt energetic every day. I really never did feel weak after those first two weeks."

Wanee decided to go home and test her new lifestyle. At this writing three months have gone by. She drops in for a visit from time to time to assure us she is maintaining her weight loss.

"I'm surprised that the fattening foods I used to eat don't tempt me anymore. I don't even want them," she tells us.

Wanee hasn't gone back to work yet. She plans to come back to MHPC and lose another 44 pounds first.

"But when I do go back and they give me the job, I'm going to accept it and then resign," she says with a laugh. "That will be my revenge."

STORY 7:

Gisela's Crusade

isela eyed her husband, a confirmed couch potato, as he lay on the sofa in front of the TV, watching his favorite hockey team. She started to speak, then hesitated. *It's no use,* she thought. *He'd just laugh at me. He'd never go. And even if he did, he'd never change.* She picked up her keys and buttoned her coat.

"You're going out again?" he asked absently, eyes fixed on the game.

"Oh, Dieter, I wish you'd come with me! You'd enjoy it, really." Her emotions welled up inside her. "You'd be surprised—it isn't anything like you think!"

"Me? Drive 60 miles in weather like this to a *health* lecture? I listen to stuff like that all the time on TV and read it in the paper."

"But it never does any good. It doesn't change anything." Gisela's face flushed, and she was near tears. "You're going to die if you don't change your lifestyle! Please, *please,* go with me just once—tonight!"

A long moment passed.

"If you come with me tonight, I promise I'll never mention it again." Gisela spoke with more confidence than she felt.

To her surprise, Dieter got up, flicked off the tube, and went for his coat. They walked to the car.

"Remember my first night?" Gisela asked. "I really didn't feel like going either. Ada and Walter had invited me to go with them. I decided it wouldn't hurt to go once, anyway."

"And then you became Gisela, the crusader." Dieter's tone was half-mocking, half-teasing.

The second night Gisela had driven her own car and persuaded three girlfriends to go with her. "Well, you'll see. My friends are as excited as I am," she defended herself.

"You know what I think? I think you've all been brainwashed," Dieter scoffed. "Nobody—*but nobody*—is going to talk me out of my salami."

An hour later the carful of excited women and one doubtful man pulled into the parking lot. People were coming from all directions.

"I had no idea it was such a big thing," Dieter mumbled as

Meet the Fun People!

Gisela pulled him along to the front row. "Hey, do we have to sit way up here?"

"Just tonight," she said, settling into a seat directly in front of the podium.

Gisela kept her promise, but Dieter didn't need to be invited again. He didn't miss a meeting for the rest of the seminar. Every night the couple and their friends drove the 60 miles from their home in Kelowna to the city of Vernon, and then drove the 60 miles home again. Dieter became as enthusiastic as Gisela.

The couple plunged wholeheartedly into the "Live With All Your Heart" diet and exercise program. In six weeks they had each lost 14 pounds. Dieter was able to stop the diuretic medication he'd been taking for high blood pressure. His doctor told him that as long as he followed his new lifestyle, he probably wouldn't need the medication.

To the amused smiles of her coworkers, Gisela gives a health lecture to each customer who comes to the popular hairdressing salon she and Deiter operate in Kelowna. But she delivers it with such charm that they take it good-naturedly. Several of them even call her "Dr. Gisela."

"In the past, I would simply dress my customers' hair," she explains. "But now I fix up their hair *and* their arteries." Gisela's eyes twinkle. "Last week I gave a talk at the local Weight Watchers Club. *Me!* Can you imagine? I told them how dieting used to be my life—one diet, then another, and another. Now I don't diet at all. I eat the right foods—the ones that are good for me. I'm actually eating more now than before, but I'm losing weight, about two pounds a week, almost like magic."

Gisela radiates her new enthusiasm. At the open house she and a friend hold once a week, Gisela shares her set of seminar tapes with her neighbors. The group has grown to 40 people, and plans are underway to move to a local church.

Gisela sums things up. "Nothing better has ever happened to us." She looks at Dieter, and he reaches for her hand. "Our marriage is better, our spiritual lives are growing, and we just feel great!"

Author's Note: Gisela was one of the more than 1,500 people who attended Dr. Hans Diehl's "Live With All Your Heart" Community Medicine Seminar in Vernon, British Columbia.

STORY 8:

Reclaiming the Recluse

With her blond curls, blue eyes, and peaches-and-cream complexion, Ruth Ashley would make a smashing Avon representative—except that she weighs 370 pounds.

"It's a miracle I'm here," she told me that first day. "I rarely go anywhere. I dread leaving my house. I haven't shopped for groceries in 10 years. I feel depressed, helpless, useless, and out of control. I often long to die. And I'm only 49 years old."

I could hardly believe what I was hearing. The woman was beautiful, immaculately groomed, and attractively dressed. She knew her colors. (It wasn't until much later that I learned she was an artist.)

"Life hasn't been kind to me," she continued, "and the one way I fight back is with food. At first I was overweight, then obese, and eventually dangerously so. I tried about every diet that came out. I was a living yo-yo—lose some, gain more, then lose and gain again. I've probably lost around 1,000 pounds altogether.

"Feeling very desperate, I had an intestinal bypass operation in 1976. The weight went fast then—too fast. After I'd lost nearly 100 pounds, the surgery was reversed to save my life. In the next few years I gained all the lost weight back, plus 50 pounds extra.

"At the beginning of this summer angina pains started, my blood pressure was up, and I felt too weak to walk or do much of anything. I isolated myself, not only from people, but from God. I was angry and thought I didn't care anymore."

> **Sometimes I'm tempted to feel I'm wasting my time in trying to help overweight people, because the results seem so dismal. Then I think of Ruth.**

But Ruth didn't isolate herself at NEWSTART—she soaked up everything around her for the next three weeks. She made new friends as people responded to her natural friendliness. She loved the food and managed to walk a little farther every day.

At the end of the program this is what she told me: "The very best result of all for me was finding my loving, caring Saviour again. No longer will I need to feel lonely, deserted, or forsaken. I now have a Friend who will always be with me and will never leave me. He was actually there all the time, but I didn't realize it. The fear is gone. My heart is full of love, joy, and peace. I have truly been reborn."

Note: Ruth followed up on her commitment to the Lord and was baptized a few months later. She is still a faithful pen pal, and we've kept in touch over the years. Her weight is a constant struggle. She will get along fine for a number of months, but a crisis always seems to come along to throw her off balance.

Sometimes I'm tempted to feel I'm wasting my time in trying to help these excessively overweight people, because the results seem so dismal. Then I think about Ruth. She may be as heavy as ever, but she has truly been reborn into a new life. No longer is she a depressed recluse, imprisoning herself in her home. It took a while to change some of her habits, but she has succeeded. Here is a portion of her latest letter, written in December 1995:

I'm doing just fine. Will be flying to Little Rock, Arkansas [from California], to be with two of my children over Christmas.

"My life is very full. I still faithfully attend TOPS [Taking Off Pounds Sensibly—an organization similar to Weight Watchers] and have many friends there, as well as at church. I weigh 370 pounds. Went up to 393, my highest weight ever. I do care. I do want to be healthy. I really try. I don't understand why I seem to be stuck in this condition.

STORY 9

Never Give In!

What is in your genes at birth will come around again in your jeans at the prime of life.—Erma Bombeck.

I've heard the story at least 100 times. The great Winston Churchill stands up to address a large body of graduating students and says in thundering tones, "Never give in, never give in, never, never, never, never." And then he sits down.

While Winston Churchill's life exemplified his message,

most of the rest of us stumble over it. Those words, however, pop an experience into my mind that must be carved in granite somewhere in memory's storehouse.

Off and on during the years I have taught weight-control classes as a hobby, not as part of my work. My interest comes from my own battle with the problem. In the early 1960s while I was a missionary doctor in Bangkok, Thailand, I held one such class. Ruby, "The Soda Pop Girl" (see Story 2 in this section), was in that class, as well as Jean, another missionary woman who was about my age.

Like many women, Jean packed quite a bit of extra weight around her hips. And like most women, she hated it and wanted to get rid of it. She believed in the program, stuck with it to the end, and did her best to cooperate. But Jean also had a skinny husband, four growing boys with ravenous appetites, and her job as a Bible worker. And she had a full-time cook. She was crestfallen when she realized she had lost only five pounds during the three months of the class.

Years later I had just about reached the end of my patience with weight-control classes. Surely there were more productive things I could do with my talents. About this time I attended a reunion of Thailand missionaries. Jean was there, and as I approached, she executed a graceful pirouette.

"See?" she said with a smile as bright as the rising sun. "I did it! After 30 years I finally got serious about my health, and those 35 pounds are gone!"

I was stunned, speechless. A long-buried dream had come true before my eyes.

"You see, Aileen," she went on, "you must never give in to discouragement. It may take some of us longer, but we don't forget."

THE FAMILY CIRCUS® By Bil Keane

7-30

"Bless this food that has been repaired for us."

Healing That Can't Be Explained:

What About Miracles?

*The prayer of faith will save the sick, and the Lord will raise
them up; and anyone who has committed sins will be forgiven.
—James 5:15, NRSV.*

I've been a Seventh-day Adventist physician for many years
and have been present at a number of prayer and anointing
services. But the only two people I've been involved with who experienced sudden and otherwise unexplainable healing are the
people whose stories I've recorded here.

Both of these events occurred during a NEWSTART program, but trust in God is the only NEWSTART principle that
can account for what happened.

What constitutes a miracle in today's world? Instant physical healing? Slower healing, which utilizes the medical knowledge God has given us? Or perhaps healing that comes in
response to the uprooting of harmful habits and indulgences?
Spiritual healing? Emotional healing?

I believe God uses all of these ways. But regardless of what
else happens, the Bible says that the prayed-for person receives
immediate forgiveness of sins and the assurance of salvation. If
the "raising up" doesn't occur on earth, it will take place when
Jesus comes.

Both people in these stories were committed Christians, and
both had been anointed as suggested in James 5:14 and 15.

Feeling Fit

STORY 1:

Whether Awake or Asleep

I had been at Weimar a year and a half when the legendary Bill Barclay came back. He'd been back only a week when my son died. Bill hugged me when he met me walking numbly across the campus. His damp eyes were gentle as he whispered, "He's only asleep for a moment. When his eyes open again, he will see Jesus. That's the promise in 1 Thessalonians 5:10."

His compassion touched me deeply. Bill was a "people person," and this kind of reaching out to others was the essence of his life. He was also a man of action. Though I can't verify it, I suspect he was born with his "motor" running at top speed. He rarely slowed down, never really stopped, never knew the meaning of "quit," and never ran out of ideas for things to do. Among other things, he sold Christian books, wrote poetry, taught school, authored books (including a daily devotional book), and served many years as an ordained minister.

But one day his nonstop lifestyle ground to a halt. He could no longer ignore the severe pain in his chest, and he underwent open-heart surgery. This ordeal relieved his pain for only one month. Repeat angiograms revealed that the remaining blood vessels were too small for further surgery. He was sent home and told to "take it easy" and "take your medicines."

Bill had no idea of how to take things easy. He fought his pain, but it was a losing battle. When someone told him that Weimar Institute was opening its NEWSTART Health Conditioning Center on May 8, 1978, Bill and his wife, Nora, applied for the first class. By this time Bill's chest pain was severe and nearly constant. It was a desperate move, but it gave them a ray of hope.

One week before the program was to begin, Bill's courage wavered. "I can't go," he told Nora. "I know I can't stand the trip. I need a shot of Demerol just to get to the bathroom."

With tears streaming down her cheeks, Nora realized how hopeless the situation seemed and spent time in her closet that night on her knees.

The next morning Bill announced, "Let's go! But we'd better start now. It's going to take a while to get there."

He rested and took his medicines while Nora packed the car.

What About Miracles?

Then they started driving. They would travel as far as Bill could endure, then stop and rest in a motel. It took three days to cover the 500 miles to the gates of the health center. As they drove in, Bill's courage nosedived. Gazing at the series of older buildings that had obviously been neglected for years, he exclaimed, "If the finest scientific minds in one of our country's best university hospitals agree that no more can be done for me, we must be out of our minds to expect anything from this primitive, forlorn little reject out in the boondocks."

But Nora's gentle reasoning prevailed: "We've come this far. What do we have to lose?"

The doctors and nurses examined Bill with sinking hearts. Realizing the desperate seriousness of his condition, they sent urgent messages upward. "Dear God, You know we have come to work here in faith. We've opened this place for You, to help people learn to live within Your plans. This man is going to die any minute now. Why, Lord? Why did You bring him here?"

Realizing the desperate seriousness of Bill's condition, doctors and nurses sent up urgent messages. By Friday night it was obvious the end was near.

That first week, despite every loving treatment and ministry that could be given, Bill's condition remained precarious. By Friday night it was obvious that the end was near. Breathing oxygen, Bill rested lightly with the help of Demerol and Valium. Nora joined the doctors and nurses as they knelt around his bed, acknowledging their total helplessness in the face of such advanced disease. They placed Bill in God's hands and prayed that His will would be done.

Bill awoke early the next morning and walked to the window to watch the sunrise. No pain. He dressed and went outside. Still no pain. There was great rejoicing and thanksgiving that day to the heavenly Healer for the miracle that had been wrought.

Bill continued to improve. As he carefully followed the strict health regime that is based on God's natural remedies, he gained strength. Each day he could breathe a little easier and walk a little farther. At the end of his 26-day stay he returned home happy, pain-free, walking two miles a day, and totally rededicated to his heavenly Father.

Bill filled the next three years to the brim. He faithfully walked from five to seven miles a day and carefully regulated his diet. His cheeks grew ruddy, his form erect, and his footsteps firm. He began to preach again, filling some pulpit nearly every Sabbath. He led out in other meetings, too, crisscrossing southern California and parts of other states. He filled in for vacationing pastors and spent hours on the telephone, sharing his knowledge of health, his new way of life, and God's great love and care for him.

Time flew by. His nitroglycerin tablets disintegrated from neglect. His constant cheerful optimism and his ready wit and sense of humor made him many new friends. He was a welcomed addition to any group.

Two years passed, then Bill had an accident with his car. Though he was not seriously injured, the ensuing legal battles and settlement hassles took a toll on his strength. Lifelong habits of operating with a "wide-open throttle" proved hard to break. One day after an especially happy but strenuous weekend of meetings and speaking engagements, his chest pain returned. From that time he felt himself slipping. Despite several hospitalizations and the insertion of a pacemaker, the pain could not be relieved.

One day Nora said, "Bill, let's go back to Weimar." Friends and loved ones agreed. God had worked one miracle there. Might there be another? So Bill and Nora joined the September 1981 NEWSTART class. Since they had been following the program nearly 100 percent for the past three years, the staff were somewhat at a loss to know what more to do for Bill. But the freedom from stress he experienced, the warm friendships renewed, the leisurely sunbaths, the fresh air, and the many prayers again blessed Bill. His pain lessened. He talked, joked, laughed, ate his saltless food, and gradually began walking again. He befriended other patients, students, and staff. He encouraged the disheartened, listened to their problems, shared their pain, and rejoiced at their triumphs.

The day of my son's funeral, Bill couldn't bring himself to attend. He sent Nora "to represent us." But knowing Bill, I was sure he was out somewhere in nature praying for me and my family. Soon after awakening the following morning, Bill experienced a serious stroke. He gradually lapsed into a coma and died seven days later at a nearby hospital.

I called Nora later at her home. "I'm so glad we came back to the health center," she said. "Bill was so happy there. God had given him those three extra years, and they were very, very special to him. To the utmost of his ability, Bill lived out his love and appreciation for the One who died for him, so that whether he is awake or asleep when Jesus comes, he has the promise of living together with Him throughout eternity [1 Thess. 5:10]. Bill was ready. That's what matters. That's what comforts me now."

See Appendix 1 for a summary of the NEWSTART lifestyle, and Appendix 2 for details of the reversal diet.

STORY 2:

Praying for a Miracle
by Alice Weisz

Three years ago during a "manipulation" I experienced excruciating pain, passed out, and awoke with severe neck pain and a loud buzzing sound in my head. The buzzing continued nonstop for two years, 24 hours a day, seven days a week. I had to keep the radio or some other kind of noise going much of the time to try to drown out the loud, continuous sound. I often felt I couldn't endure it, that I'd go out of my mind.

During that time I spent thousands of dollars on specialists, X-rays, CAT scans, angiograms—anything that might lead to relief. Finally I was advised to enter the pain clinic at the University of California at Davis's Medical School to learn to live with the condition.

I received the application and a questionnaire of more than 900 questions. I looked at that endless list of questions and thought about the time and expense ahead. And for what? My courage failed, and I wept in discouragement.

Then the phone rang. It was my daughter. When I explained my plight, she said, "Mom, forget the pain clinic and go to a NEWSTART program."

So I did. When I got there and explained my situation to the doctor, I told her this was my last hope, truly, my *desperation station.* I could see immediately that I must have said the wrong thing. She became very distressed and tactfully tried to explain to me that the NEWSTART program did not "cure" things such as I had. She told me that all they could do for me was to put me on an optimal general health program and ask the Lord's blessing, committing my life and problem into His hands. I told her that was OK with me. Whatever happened, I would accept the consequences. If healing came, I would be grateful. If not, with God's help, I would live with it.

I plunged into every detail of the program, 100 percent. I attended the classes, ate the food, walked the trails, worked in the garden, took my treatments. And the problem continued, unabated. But I wasn't discouraged. I loved everything. I knew the staff was praying for me, and the other patients prayed for me too. Healed or not, I was determined to make this a mountaintop experience in my life.

On the eighth day, after my regular physical therapy treatment, it seemed that the noise was decreasing. But I had to rush up to hydrotherapy and didn't think too much about it. As I lay on the hydro table receiving my water treatment, I realized the noise had changed—I could barely hear it. Also, the neck pain was gone. But I was cautious at first, a bit fearful that perhaps it was only a temporary phenomenon.

> **All they could do was to put me on an optimal general health program asking the Lord's blessing, committing my life and problem to Him.**

Within the hour, though, I was convinced that a miracle had happened. And there was rejoicing and praising the Lord and dancing over the trails of the Sierra Nevadas such as I envisioned David must have done after his great victory in battle, when he came dancing before the Lord into Jerusalem!

More than a year has passed since that day. I remain free of the noise, the pressure, and the neck pain. I continue to practice every health principle the Lord has given me as completely as I can. Since He chose to heal me through the vehicle of the NEWSTART lifestyle, I'm dedicated to continuing it for life. No way do I wish to return to my previous miserable state!

Every day is a joy to me, and I cannot praise and thank God enough. I want to share this story with the whole world.

Author's Note: Three years later I met Alice again. She was still rejoicing over her healing.

What About Miracles?

"But I have to tell you something else," she confided. "My health and energy are better now than at any time in my life." She paused, and with a hint of a giggle added, "On a recent 11-mile trek into Yosemite, a group of young people wanted a picture of this 74-year-old, white-haired mountaineer. 'When I get old,' one girl told me, 'I want to be like you.'"

Church Leaders and NEWSTART:

A Fishbowl Life

Lifestyle is as religious as washing our teeth. Salvation doesn't depend on washing our teeth, but we do it anyway.
—Contributed.

What if you lived in a fishbowl, with people watching what you ate, how you dressed, where you went, and what you did? It would be an unbearable burden. Yet how often we Christians do such things to our pastors and leaders, even though we know better.

Still, there are appropriate times to seek guidance. While the church is strengthened by active lay members and independent ministries, there are always a few who seek church support for their personal agendas. Others start out with a good idea, but carry it to extremes.

Because Weimar Institute began offering a different kind of health care than was available in conventional Seventh-day Adventist hospitals, church leaders found themselves in a precarious situation. Was this type of care a return to our roots, to the kind of medical care Ellen White encouraged in her time? Was it appropriate for the present time? Or was this yet another attempt to advance extreme and unbalanced methods?

At first Adventist leaders watched and waited. In time some came to "taste and see" for themselves. Here are a few of their stories.

Feeling Fit

STORY 1:

Beating Burnout
by J. Robert Spangler

I'll admit I was prejudiced. Extremists, I suspected. Maybe even fanatical. Certainly legalistic. A bunch of health nuts. But a close friend kept urging me to go to this Seventh-day Adventist health center in California.

"Take some time off and give it a try," he said. "What do you have to lose?"

I guess I didn't have much to lose. I felt lousy and woke up tired. I was stressed, weary, and depressed. I was losing interest in life, a situation that was entirely out of character for me. All my life I had worked hard and thrived on it. I had certainly never been bored. My life had always been challenging, exciting, and fulfilling. So what was the matter now? Perhaps I was burned out. Maybe this was the signal, the way it felt when it was time to quit. My friend knew I was giving serious thought to retirement. After all, I was nearly 65 and had 44 years of service on my record. My friend also knew that I hated the thought of quitting.

I struggled on for another three months. But I was definitely over the hill and going down the other side. Vacations didn't help, and hospital admission was out of the question. Finally my wife, Marie, and I signed on for a 25-day live-in program. Actually, I believed in what Weimar stood for. I had been reared in a Seventh-day Adventist home. I had lived the Adventist health message, including vegetarianism, my entire life. I often taught health principles, and my wife gave cooking demonstrations. I was sure I knew it all. What more could I do? True, I was quite a bit overweight and had an understandable human weakness for desserts, but was that enough to bring a man down?

When we arrived, it was like stepping into another world. Suddenly freed from the pressures and stresses of our work, we literally melted into the arms of the loving, caring, dedicated, and talented staff. Was this their secret ingredient?

Our first meal, however, was a shocker and restored my suspicions. We felt like King Nebuchadnezzar of Daniel's day, who, after losing his reason, began eating grass! Was it necessary for food to be so tasteless? The food was all—and I mean *all*—unrefined. Because even orange and apple juices are refined, we were taught to get our juice in its natural form—from the whole fruit. NEWSTART cooks use no animal products, such as milk, cheese, or eggs. They use little salt and no condiments, extracted oils, grease, or refined sugars in preparing the food.

After about a week, we decided they must have changed cooks, because the food tasted decidedly better. And by the end of our 25-day stay, we were actually relishing the plain, unadulterated food. It was a real eye-opener to realize how far we, a conservative, conscientious Seventh-day Adventist couple, had strayed from eating natural food, simply prepared.

Exercise was the next most important factor to impact us newcomers. Most of us know we need exercise, but few of us really understand the enormous difference it can make in our health and well-being. Marie and I were soon doing more than five miles a day, walking in the sunshine and fresh air of the Sierra Nevadas.

Many other benefits came our way as well, such as relaxing hydrotherapy treatments, increased time to study God's word, the devotionals, and the beautiful prayers of persons ministering to us.

> **Most of us know we need exercise, but few of us really understand the enormous difference it can make in our health and well-being.**

NEWSTART is an acronym representing the eight health principles Ellen White writes about in *The Ministry of Healing*—nutrition, exercise, water, sunshine, temperance, air, rest, and trust in God. The genius of this program is found in the marvelous blending together of every element that touches life. The focus of the NEWSTART lifestyle center was not only to revive us, but to teach us a way of life we could take home and continue to live for the rest of our lives. To that end, we were gently instructed in the whys and hows of a healthy lifestyle with practical cooking demonstrations and scientific, yet understandable, lectures by physicians.

The results were not only good, they were astounding! After only two weeks I felt like a new man. By the fourth week I was my old self again—energetic, optimistic, creative, and on fire. I could hardly wait to get back to my work.

It's been nearly 10 years now since our NEWSTART experience, and I've retained most of my gains. I'm 32 pounds lighter, and I walk three to five miles a day. And I, admittedly the weakest of the weak when it comes to food, have been able to make some major changes. For one thing, we have cut out dairy products. Besides lowering my dangerously high cholesterol level and helping me lose weight, this change has relieved me of the stuffed-up nose I had suffered from for years. What a joy to breathe freely once more and to feel good every new day!

Looking back, I view my time at NEWSTART as experiencing Adventism at it's best. The program consists of many threads tightly woven into a pattern of beauty. The entire staff, including students, contribute to this fabric. Threads of prayer, encouragement, scientific evidence, practice, fellowship, and study are all woven together into the healing process.

The queen of Sheba, after seeing for herself how God had blessed Israel under King Solomon, declared, "I did not believe the words until I came and saw with my own eyes; and indeed the half was not told me" (1 Kings 10:7, NKJV). That's the way Marie and I feel about the NEWSTART program.

Retire? Don't be ridiculous! Yes, I have retired, but only from a full-time salary. I am still going strong, working for our cablevision program, *It Is Written*. I would rather die with my boots on; but until then, I plan to concentrate on doing what I love most—writing and preaching.

STORY 2:

Moment of Truth
by Lincoln Steed

I guess I asked for it. I'd been feeling a little stressed out, and I thought it was time for a checkup.

"Are you going to be all right?" asked the nurse, a little too solicitously for my liking, as she strapped my arm and drew near with the needle. "I mean, you're not going to faint, are you?"

Not from the pain, that was for sure. But the anticipation of a bad result always makes me less than an ideal patient. Nobody fainted at my blood-taking. It was all very undramatic, and they promised to call me when the results were in. Actually,

A Fishbowl Life

I called them—several times— trying to find out the state of my body. However, I wasn't prepared for the call I received a few days later.

"Your cholesterol of 258 mg/% [6.6 mmol/l] is very high," said the nurse. "The doctor wants you to begin medication immediately to get it down to more ideal levels of 150 to 170 [3.9 to 4.4 mmol/l]."

I walked to the pharmacy to pick up my medicine. (Exercise is necessary to keep cholesterol moving, right? Well, wrong reasoning, actually, but a good start.) And I started taking those little pills every day, without fail.

The moment of truth came after my return from the doctor's office, where I had picked up a pharmaceutical company giveaway. On the back I found a food chart giving cholesterol and fat contents for a wide range of basic foodstuffs and prepared meals. It wasn't the first time I had seen such a chart, but this time I looked at it more closely. That's when something struck me with the force of a revelation. Clearly, some foods are higher in cholesterol and fat than others. But the bottom-line reality is that fruits, grains, and vegetables have no cholesterol, are very low in fat, and high in certain fibers that help lower the blood cholesterol.

It's amazing how fixated we consumers have become on foods low in fat and cholesterol. We have all become inveterate food label readers. All the while the answer is staring us in the face. Back to basics! It's not a bad idea, especially dietwise. Thousands of years ago the ideal diet was spelled out by our Creator. The Bible says God told Adam and Eve, "I have given you every plant yielding seed which is upon the face of all the earth, and every tree with seed in its fruit; you shall have them for food" (Gen. 1:29, RSV).

It's been only four weeks since that moment of truth. Yesterday I had another blood test. The result was terrific: my cholesterol was down to 124 mg/% [3.2 mmol/l]! My doctor took me off the cholesterol-lowering drug, saying, "You don't need this anymore. Your diet change certainly made a difference. Stay with it, and you won't have to worry about drug side effects, seeing the pharmacist, or seeing me!" Great news!

More good news is that I've lost weight, gained energy, regained an incredible taste appreciation for simpler foods, and, very important, I'm feeling much better. What a way to be!

Author's Note: It had been a year since Lincoln gave us his story, so I phoned him at his office in May 1996.

Feeling Fit

"I'm doing fine," he reassured me. "My weight is what it was when I got married, which means I'm 30 pounds lighter. I only regret I didn't start this lifestyle sooner. I feel years younger."

STORY 3:

Fourteen Extra Years
by Father Fergus McGuinness

About three months after my triple coronary bypass, it was all there again—the pain, the fatigue, the frustration. I returned to the doctor.

"The surgery has helped you some, but that is as far as we can go," he said. "Continue your medications and try to control your stress. Maybe you should go see a psychiatrist."

His words thudded upon my weary ears and discouraged heart. I had thrown away the medications I had been gobbling by the handful prior to surgery. Did I have to start that old routine again? When I had trouble sleeping, I was told to try a few drinks. It worked, but I kept needing to drink more and more. The double fear of returning to my medications—and possibly facing alcoholism—was too much for my nervous system.

But before I had a nervous breakdown, I found a NEW-START program. There I learned what to eat (and when) and the value of exercise. It took considerable discipline to discard old lifetime patterns and to adopt health-building habits. But by the end of 25 days I'd lost 17 pounds, dropped my cholesterol 100 mg/% [2.6 mmol/l], and my triglycerides 300 mg/% [7.8 mmol/l]. I felt 10 years younger.

Author's Note: I had a letter from Father McGuinness in 1995. Here's what he had to say:

"What I learned at NEWSTART has added 14 years to my life. I've been at least 70 percent faithful to what I have learned. I'm now 74 years old and work every day. I have no plans to retire."

STORY 4:

The Preacher Finds a NEWSTART
by H.M.S. Richards, Jr.

My story begins at one of our monthly Voice of Prophecy board of directors meetings. Having just returned from an extended trip (and having to catch up on the pile of correspondence), I was not looking forward to the all-day meeting. Sitting next to me that morning was my dear friend, the late Dr. Vernon Foster. He could see that I was under pressure, and he also noticed my girth.

"How much do you weigh now?" he asked, as we chatted between agenda items.

I was embarrassed to tell him I was up to 245 pounds. I was just too busy to exercise much, and the weight was going up. Over lunch that day Dr. Foster became the preacher. He reminded me of the importance of God's workers being in the best physical condition possible, and he went on to tell me about Weimar Institute's NEWSTART program.

"Harold," he concluded, "you really need to experience the NEWSTART program. It will save your life and give you many more years of service."

Well, I wasn't too sure about going to such a place. I was much too busy to take the time off, so I made excuses.

"Listen," Dr. Foster said firmly, "don't worry about a thing. I'll see when the next program begins and let you know."

Not wanting to hurt his feelings, I reluctantly said OK. Over the next few days I began to think. *Lord, the Bible says even You and Your disciples took time to "go apart and rest a while." Is this what I need?* Looking back, I know the Lord was leading me to this place. As I drove through the gates of the institute, weariness, fatigue, guilt, and discouragement nearly overcame me. When I got to my room and sat down, I shed a few tears.

But not for long. NEWSTART is a busy place. I was introduced to those who would be going through the same program—a delightful group composed of businesspeople, homemakers, physicians, and a young woman just getting off drugs. Gentle, loving people guided us through the details of the program—fresh air, sunshine, simple food, gallons of water, time to rest, hikes on beautiful mountain trails, and hydrotherapy! I finally began to calm down and relax.

I called my wife, Mary, and told her all about the program, including how many calories I was assigned each day. I told her I didn't think I could last very long on so few calories. But surprisingly, just the opposite was true. I discovered I would be filled up with delicious food, homemade breads, and fruits, and still not reach my assigned calories! To my delight, I noticed my weight coming down.

One day my physician told me to drop all my blood pressure medicine. I asked him if he was sure. "Yes," he replied, "now is the time. Don't take any tonight, then see me in the morning." The next morning in his office I couldn't believe it when he took my blood pressure—120/60! Better yet, my attitudes and perspectives began to change. I began to understand that just as God gave us spiritual and moral laws that were meant to be followed, He'd given us health laws, too. Many workers in the prime of life have been cut down before their time for not following the simple laws of good health.

The classes were precious. Dr. Sang Lee's lecture on cardiovascular stress turned out to be a beautiful presentation on righteousness by faith. I wish you could have seen the faces of our class members—the industrialist, the three physicians, the former drug user—all of us in tears. We left the classroom quietly. I went to my room and knelt down beside my bed and gave my heart to Jesus again!

I did find a new start! Those few days spent learning about the combination of exercise and rest, healthy food and time for spiritual growth, have been most important to me during the nearly 10 years that have followed.

How much do I weigh now? One hundred ninety-five pounds! Yes, I am the preacher who found NEWSTART!

Author's Note: A letter from Pastor Richards (February 1997) spoke about his rumored "heart attack": "No heart attack; just a leaky aortic valve that might need surgery down the line." He adds, "I shudder to think where I would be today if I had not had my fantastic NEWSTART experience."

STORY 5:

From Zombie to Fireball
by Pastor Fred Prichard

Medications controlled my blood pressure, but I was like a zombie. I just kind of wandered around, trying to do little things, but accomplishing nothing. The frustration was unbearable for one who had lived a very full and exciting life.

I had pioneered much of the early Seventh-day Adventist mission work in South and Central America. Even after retirement interesting challenges kept me involved. But then my weight crept up. So did diabetes. Then my blood pressure. My worried doctor ordered medicines to control my blood pressure, hoping to prevent a stroke. However, the medicine put me in an unreal daze.

Providentially, I got into a NEWSTART program. It's been a year now, and it's still hard to believe what has happened. I'm 40 pounds lighter, my blood sugars are normal without medication, and so is my blood pressure.

I feel like I've been reborn. Thank you, God and NEWSTART, for helping me out of a zombie netherworld into a vigorous reality full of exciting challenge.

NEWSTART and Aging:

How Old Is Old?

*Beautiful young people are accidents of nature. Beautiful old
people are works of art.*—Selected.

When told her fitness evaluation rated her cardiovascular
fitness level as that of a healthy 60-year-old, 90-year-old
Hulda Crooks replied, "Research indicates that a healthful
lifestyle can hold back the aging processes as much as 30 years.
Thirty extra years of good health—who could turn down a bargain like that? Well, I couldn't, and I believe I'm a living example of the truth of those words."

Octogenarian marathoner Mavis Lindgren observes, "At
89 it's a wonderful thing to get up in the morning and not hurt
anywhere."

"As a woman who is well past 65, I can tell you I'm having a
wonderful time. I have stayed in shape by exercising 45 minutes
every morning and walking whenever I can," says advice colum-
nist Ann Landers. "I've never touched cigarettes or alcohol. As
Robert Browning said, This is 'the last of life, for which the first
was made.'"

> **Research indicates that a healthful lifestyle can
> hold back the aging processes as much as 30 years.
> Thirty extra years of good health!**

And from the world of science, the latest antiaging advice:

1. Maintain clean, unplugged arteries by eating low-fat,
high-fiber food.

2. Keep the body in good repair by stimulating blood flow to
the remotest parts of the body through regular active exercise.

3. Avoid the health damage of cigarettes, alcohol, over-weight, and negative thinking.

STORY 1:

The Gun and the Bible

Doctors should realize people don't feel old, they just look that way.—Hattie Hammond.

I helped this little lump of a woman walk the few steps into my office and sit down. She looked like Mother Time—old, wrinkled, weak, tottering on her cane.

"So I lay there with a gun to my head and a Bible on my heart," Hattie told me. "I was totally miserable, and I had no more money for doctors or medicine. Would I live? or would I die? Then I decided to sell my house and come here."

Well, she had my attention! I looked at her, wondering how to go about asking what her trouble was. She read the question in my eyes and handed me a neatly printed list of her medical problems—all 12 of them. I was startled, first of all because all 12 symptoms were serious, and second, because I'd never had a patient who was quite this organized. Her step may have been unsteady, but her 84-year-old mind was as keen as mine. I wrote the 12 symptoms on her chart and introduced her to her NEWSTART program.

At the end of the 25 days she surprised me again by handing me a report of what had happened to each of her 12 problems. It read like this:

BEFORE NEWSTART	AFTER NEWSTART
1. Hypoglycemic shakes	No hypoglycemia
2. Hypertension	Blood pressure coming down
3. Obesity	Lost 10 pounds
4. Swollen legs	No more swelling
5. Painful joints	No pain in any joint
6. Constipation	No constipation
7. Urinary frequency	Get up only once at night

How Old Is Old?

8. Can't walk	Can walk one mile
9. Insomnia	Sleep well
10. Chest congestion and cough—nine years	Congestion and cough gone
11. Painful feet	No pain in feet
12. Depressed	No depression

Hattie smiled happily. "After 10 years of treatments and $50,000," she said, "I never felt as good as I did after only a few days here. I praise God for NEWSTART. I can go to church again. I'm canceling the convalescent home and going house hunting."

Mother Time had turned back the clock.

STORY 2:

I Have to Die Sometime

Without health, life is not life; it is only a state of languor and suffering—an image of death.—Rabelais.

I'm not really sure why I'm here," Margaret said. "Probably because it's my last hope. After all, I'm 79 years old, and you have to die sometime." Her ample body slumped into her chair as dejection etched the lines of her face.

"Two years ago my husband was told he was going blind, and nothing could be done about it." Her deep sigh resonated with weariness. "My own health was poor, but I kept going for his sake. When he died six months ago, I was ready to quit." She paused, searching my face for a reaction, or perhaps for a glimmer of understanding.

"You are grieving, and you must feel depressed," I said gently, leaning forward, encouraging her to continue.

"Yes, I am, and I have good reasons." She straightened up, a flicker of fire glinting her gaze. "My life is a mess. My digestion is so poor I've been eating six meals a day and still feel bloated. I have to go for colonic irrigations twice a week to eliminate properly. My blood pressure is too high, and my circulation is so poor that my ankles are swollen and discolored. I'm much too heavy. But worst of all, my back and right hip hurt so much I

69

can hardly get around. I'm taking 11 different medications, but they don't seem to do any good. I just feel so miserable that I told my daughter I was ready to join Daddy. She wanted me to come here, but I don't think much can be done for my condition."

Despite her seeming despair, Margaret gamely plunged into her program. But what about those twice weekly colonic irrigations? We didn't give those treatments at our center, and I wondered how patient she would be about waiting for her normal elimination to catch up. Many older people become obsessed with their bowels. If they miss a day, they are convinced that poisons will begin creeping into their bodies. My assurances that some people go a month without elimination (an abnormality called "megacolon") with no ill effects usually fall on deaf ears.

My concern about Margaret evaporated when she happily reported "results" the third day. Miserable or not, she was giving the program her best effort.

Three weeks later we were again in my office. This time, however, Margaret was all smiles, and her eyes were bright and alive. "I've changed my mind about my condition," she reported. "So far I've lost 13 pounds. I'm eating three meals a day with good appetite and have no more digestive problems. I've not needed a single colonic irrigation. My blood pressure has come down, and the swelling in my legs is nearly gone. The pain in my back and hip is so much improved that I can get around much better. I need to take only three medications a day now." She paused, then added with conviction, "But the best thing is my mental outlook. I feel so much better now that my problems don't seem so serious. I feel like I'm in control of my life again. Sure, I feel lonely, and I still have trouble sleeping. But I don't want to die anymore. I've got too much to live for. I can't wait to get home."

Author's Note: The stories of Margaret Friesendorf and Hattie Hammond sound too good to be true, but every detail is real. I've seen too many of these "miracles" happen to believe that anyone's condition is hopeless.

How Old Is Old?

STORY 3:

My Legs Keep Going

It's so frustrating," Mae Libby said with disgust. "I can't walk a block without my legs cramping. Is it expecting too much to want to be active and vital past age 77?"

Age 77? I did a double take. This attractive woman who looked as though she was ready to spill over with fun and energy was 77?

She clapped her hand over her mouth. "Now I've gone and done it! I didn't mean to tell you my age! Promise me you won't write it down anywhere." She tried to stare fiercely at me, but started to giggle.

I laughed too. But I knew her request was serious.

"I keep wondering if it's worth the investment to seek further medical help," she continued, composed now. "This place is pretty expensive, you know. I suppose a person has to accept a few discomforts as the years pass." She paused, locking her eyes with mine. "But I *refuse* to accept old age without a fight!"

I loved her spunkiness. "OK, let's fight! Your problem, as you probably know, is poor circulation in your legs. My problem is to find a way to correct your problem."

"You mean operate?" She was suspicious now.

"No, no, not that. Something much harder. But I can't do it for you. I'll teach you how, and then it's up to you to do it."

She looked at me quizzically, wondering if I was playing games.

"You see, there are several ways we can get more blood into your legs. One way is to put you on a diet that's very low in fat. Fat thickens the blood, and the red blood cells start sticking to each other, retarding circulation. Cleaning out excess fat from the blood increases circulation almost immediately. Second, hydrotherapy treatments will loosen up your arteries. Heat dilates arteries, and cold constricts at first, then dilates them as the blood tries to warm up the cold area. Your third assignment is exercise. Walk as far as you can, then rest when the cramps start. Do this several times a day. Exercise not only stimulates your remaining circulation, but also helps build up collateral circulation."

Mae, a minister's wife, thought she already understood and practiced all there was to know about Seventh-day Adventist health principles. Indeed, her good health and sharp mind reflected her healthy lifestyle. Her only problem was her legs. She learned the value of hydrotherapy and became far more strict with her diet, eliminating all dairy products and visible fats and oils. And she kept walking.

By the end of 25 days, Mae was walking three miles with minimal pain. She was as happy as a little girl on a merry-go-round. "My daughter is going to be very surprised when we walk through the shopping mall together, because she won't have to stop every two seconds for my leg cramps to go away."

Four years later I met Mae Libby again. "I'm still sticking to the program at least 90 percent of the time," she reported. "I am active, happy, and on the go all day long. I'm teaching a Sabbath school class and am the Community Services leader at our church. The cramps in my legs have stopped. I enjoy life and feel fine. My only regret is that so few people are open to learning about this lifestyle. Most feel they must get terribly ill before they need to change. But this is such a good life! I praise God for His blessings."

In a recent letter from her I noted with a smile that she is no longer secretive about her age: *I'm 92 years old now, and aside from annoying arthritis at times, am enjoying good health. I still carry on most of my usual pursuits, except driving my car, which I prefer not to do in today's busy traffic. I continue to praise God for restoring my health.* One of her nieces told me with a touch of awe, "Can you believe Aunt Mae goes camping with us? She is so much fun, and she tells us that she honestly doesn't feel a day over 60!"

STORY 4:

My Family All Died
by Phyllis Dickson, R.N. (pseudonym)

When my youngest brother dropped dead of a heart attack, I panicked. I totally panicked. Seven brothers and sisters have died, one by one, mostly of heart and vascular problems. My husband died too.

At age 68 I was the only one left. I had already had two heart attacks. When my last brother died, I became so upset I started having severe and sudden spells of tachycardia (rapid heart beat) and arrythmias (irregular beats). The medics would rush me to intensive care. Three or four days later I'd go home, but the same thing happened every week or two, and I knew I could die at any minute.

I saw five heart specialists. I was given several medications and told to go to bed for a year. I pleaded with God for help, then ended up in a NEWSTART program.

That was 18 months ago. Today I am off all medication, have no more angina or arrythmias, and feel full of energy and interest in life. I care for my home, paint, do volunteer work, go aerobic dancing three or four times a week, and teach a Sunday school class. I don't plan to retire until I'm 90, at least. There's too much I want to do!

Do you doubt my story? I wouldn't believe it either, except that it really happened to me.

STORY 5:

Sweetheart of the Marathon

Tiny Mavis Lindgren is a celebrity in her own right. Tired of being a pulmonary cripple with frequent hospitalizations for pneumonia, she began training at age 70. By age 85 she had run 63 marathons. I met her just after she'd turned 89. She had already run three marathons that year and was itching to do another one.

"What I'd really like to do next is run the London Marathon," she confided. "If I succeed, do you think I might get to meet Queen Elizabeth?"

That's the secret ingredient of people like Mavis Lindgren, Hulda Crooks, the Kegleys, and the Andersons. (See "Adventist Celebrities," Section 15.) They take each day a step at a time, but they never run out of dreams!

> It isn't a calamity to die
> With dreams unfulfilled, but
> It is a calamity not to dream.
> —Benjamin E. Mays

"I take this one for my allergy, and this
one for the drowsiness it causes, and
this one to calm me down after the other
one wakes me up, and . . ."

NEWSTART and Cancer:

What About Cancer Cures?

*When you pass through the waters I will be with you; and
through the rivers, they shall not overwhelm you.
—Isaiah 43:2, RSV.*

Healthful lifestyle practices can prevent 70 to 80 percent of
today's cancers. For example, if you don't smoke tobacco or
drink alcohol, you are already at 30 to 35 percent less risk than
the average North American. And if you are a vegetarian, eating little or no meat or dairy products, you can decrease your
risk by another 30 percent.

Once cancer establishes itself in the body, however, there is
no firm evidence that the NEWSTART lifestyle will do more
than maximize health and strengthen the body's ability to fight
the disease. Some cancer patients come to NEWSTART programs for this reason. Others come desiring to deepen their
spiritual relationships. Most come for both reasons, and in my
experience no one has left disappointed.

STORY 1:

I Choose Life

Life is more than food.—Luke 12:23, RSV.

We don't treat cancer at NEWSTART, so I was more than a
little surprised when I was asked to administer
chemotherapy to Marie.

Marie was quick to reassure me. "It's like this," she said. "I
was in shock when they told me I had cancer of the breast and

75

lymph nodes. When I prayed earnestly for guidance, God impressed me to take advantage of the best medical knowledge available, which in my case was surgery, followed by chemotherapy.

"I was also impressed to open my life more fully to the health knowledge God has given us. This led to my checking into a NEWSTART program. My oncologist agreed for me to receive my last two doses of chemotherapy here, because competent physicians are present to administer them."

I was relieved to know that Marie was not expecting a cancer cure. She came for two reasons: to maximize her health so that her body would have a better chance to fight the disease, and to experience a deeper spiritual relationship with her Lord. It is with an understanding of these two goals that we accept a few cancer patients into the NEWSTART programs.

Marie found what she came for. Here is an excerpt from a letter she wrote later:

It's been four years now, and I just feel wonderful. My health is better than it has ever been, my energy level is high, and there's been no sign of recurrence of the original cancer.

> **A simple, healthful, balanced lifestyle has put my body in the optimum condition to fight disease. My future is in God's hands.**

I've fully dedicated myself to the healthful lifestyle I learned, which seems to me is in beautiful harmony with God's original plans for mankind. My spiritual life and relationship with Jesus are deeper and more real than I ever dreamed possible.

Two years ago another kind of cancer reared its ugly head— a malignant melanoma. It was removed, and there are no signs of recurrence.

I know that a simple, healthful, balanced lifestyle has put my body in the optimum condition to fight disease. Whenever I am tempted to eat something harmful, I think of the text, "Life is more than food," and I choose life!

My future is in God's hands; I am unafraid and at peace.

What About Cancer Cures?

STORY 2:

The Hopeless Case

Blanche arrived from Hawaii with flowers in her hair and leis around her neck. What could be wrong with such a sparkling, vivacious young woman? It was hard to believe her story.

"For three days my stomach swelled bigger and bigger, and I gained 20 pounds. I could hardly eat—only a few bites at a time. My doctor put me in the hospital and ordered a CAT scan. When it showed a tumor, they operated right away."

Blanche had grown up in a Christian home, but her outgoing, fun-loving nature soon got her involved in the secular pleasures. Spiritual interests became less and less important. About three years ago, however, a loving Christian couple cared for her ill father for a year. Blanche felt as though they were angels and was soon studying the Bible with them and began going to church. After her baptism she became the church secretary and taught a Sabbath school class.

"Before the operation my pastor prayed with me, and I felt very peaceful. I had no fear at all," Blanche told me. "After surgery the doctor explained that I had cancer, and that it had fastened itself to my intestines, bladder, colon, uterus, peritoneum, and liver. In other words, it was inoperable. They took out one large chunk from the middle (the omentum) that was in danger of producing an obstruction. They removed all the fluid that had made my stomach so big, then sewed me up.

"My doctor was very up-front with me, which I appreciated. He said neither chemotherapy, cobalt, nor radiation would be of any real help. He gave me six months to a year, at the most. He told me to live as well as I could and to take care of myself. I was able to accept the news calmly. I felt no anger or resentment. Wasn't my life in God's hands?

"A week later the elders of my church came for a prayer and anointing service for my healing (James 5:14). I told the Lord that whatever happened was all right with me, that I put all things in His keeping.

"One beautiful blessing that resulted from this service was a reunion with my husband. We had been separated for several months, but now we are closer than we ever have been.

"I had heard about this NEWSTART program. I know you

don't claim to cure cancer here, but you do teach a lifestyle in harmony with God's natural remedies. Since I put my life in God's hands, I want to learn all I can about His way of life."

Three weeks after her surgery Blanche arrived at NEW-START. She loved the trees, and even the food! "It's so natural, so like God produced it," she said.

The next morning, feeling a little homesick, Blanche felt the tears coming. She found a little chapel and knelt there as the sobs came faster. She continued crying, harder and harder. Then the storm stopped. *OK, that's enough self-pity,* she told herself. She asked God for strength and for cheerfulness. "I felt a great relief; my happy spirit returned. Then I realized that this was the first time I'd been able to cry since hearing the news of my cancer," she said.

> **I know you don't claim to cure cancer here, but you do teach a lifestyle in harmony with God's natural remedies.**

"My NEWSTART days went by like a dream. I learned how to care for my body, how to strengthen my immune system. My abdomen stayed soft and became less tender. I had a good appetite and ate all I wanted."

Blanche's husband kept streams of beautiful leis and exotic tropical flowers flowing into the lodge, and she shared them with everyone.

When it came time to leave, Blanche told us she would be homesick for her friends at NEWSTART. "But I'm going home feeling personally closer to my Lord than ever before. My illness has already opened the way for me to talk to many of my friends about God. If just one soul is brought to Jesus through my experience, it will be worth it all."

Blanche died peacefully a few months later, safe in Jesus.

What About Cancer Cures?

STORY 3:

Thank God for Cancer!

Often the test of courage is not to die, but to live.
—Conto Vittorio Alfiere.

What? You welcomed cancer?" I thought I'd heard everything, but this was a new one. "But why? After AIDS, cancer is the most dreaded disease in the world!"

Carol (not her real name) gave it to me straight. "I've lived a very self-destructive lifestyle. For years I haven't cared about my health. I've smoked since my early teens, and I drank heavily for a long time. My life seemed so empty and worthless that I began to wish I could die. When the doctors told me, after lung surgery, that they'd found cancer, I actually felt relief. The sooner I died, the better. I couldn't think of anything I wanted to live for.

So why was she here at NEWSTART? She wasn't shy about sharing her reasons.

"I was raised a strict Roman Catholic and spent four years in a convent. But I was rebellious, and when my 23-year-old brother gave me a cigarette, I not only smoked it, I continued to smoke. I also began dating, but I mostly sat around smoking with the boys. I was 14 years old.

"At age 18 I married a struggling young medical student. I was a talented singer and got a job singing with the St. Louis municipal opera for four years. My earnings helped put my husband through medical school.

"As time went by, problems mounted, and my husband began drinking. When our marriage deteriorated, I followed his example. By the time I was 38 I was a divorced woman with three children to finish raising. I held various jobs—secretary, photographer, and bar owner.

"Two years later I married an engineer. He was a good provider, and I had everything I needed materially. But I couldn't seem to find myself, to find my place in life. My husband's dominant nature and overprotectiveness smothered me. I longed for some recognition in life other than just being a servant to John.

"My alcoholism worsened to the point that I had a seizure

five years ago and spent three days in a coma. I quit drinking, not because I wanted to live, but because as long as I had to live, I didn't want to be crippled or lose my mind.

"But my smoking increased. I often sat up far into the night, smoking cigarettes and drinking coffee. I developed a chronically worsening case of bronchitis, an ulcer, and finally, angina pains. My blood pressure went sky-high, and I had a small stroke. Despite all of this, I never seriously tried to stop smoking. Even after lung cancer surgery, I just didn't care."

"Wasn't your family pretty upset by this time?" I asked.

"Yes, but they felt helpless, because they didn't know what to do for me. One of my husband's employees had gone through a NEWSTART program. He told me I could find a whole new way of life at this place. By that time I was so depressed and sick that I actually began to want help. When my husband offered to come with me, I decided to come. But I'm scared. I have no idea what I'm getting into."

At first Carol told us she only wanted to cut down her smoking. But by the second day she felt sufficiently encouraged and supported to make the break—cold turkey.

> **My most valuable things were freedom from angina pain and reconnection with God who cares and wants me physically and spiritually whole.**

The next five days were full of misery. Constant nausea, punctuated by vomiting, reactivated her ulcer. Her stomach hurt terribly. The headaches didn't let up. Her blood pressure reached 230/100. But she didn't quit—she stuck it out. Here is how she described the experience.

"The NEWSTART staff stayed right with me. I was tenderly and lovingly cared for. I had lots of water treatments, consisting of fomentations, whirlpool, and cooling baths. I drank 20 cups of water a day. Gradually the withdrawal symptoms subsided. By the sixth day my blood pressure was back to normal, and I slept nine hours straight for the first time in five years!"

As the nicotine and carbon monoxide washed out of her system, more oxygenated blood reached her heart, and the angina faded. Before she left, she was walking five miles without pain. She was able to stop all six of her medicines. She lost so much weight that she could barely hold her pants up.

"It's hard to realize how miserable and depressed I was just three weeks ago," Carol told me. "My life is so different now. The craving for cigarettes is gone. My whole outlook has changed. My husband is delighted!

"What's surprising," she continued, "is that the most valuable thing I found at NEWSTART was not freedom from my smoking habit, nor the ability to hike trails without angina pain. It was reconnecting with a God who cares and who wants me to be both physically and spiritually whole. I am hopeful now. I have a reason to live. I have finally found the way to fill that empty void in my life.

"Yes, I can still honestly say I thank God for my cancer, not because I want to die, but because it led me to a new life with Him."

NEWSTART and Hypertension:

The Lowdown on High Blood Pressure

Did you know that blood pressure can go up when a person is excited, stressed, nervous, angry, or experiencing some other emotional stimulation? That is why blood pressure needs to be checked several times before it can be determined that disease is present.

Hypertension is the medical term for high blood pressure. Hypertension is diagnosed when the systolic blood pressure reading (top number) is consistently over 140 and/or the diastolic reading (lower number) is 90 or above.

THE BAD NEWS

A person with high blood pressure is three times more likely to have a heart attack, five times more likely to develop heart failure, and eight times more likely to suffer a stroke than persons with normal blood pressure. Hypertension is called the "silent" disease, because there are no warning symptoms until a stroke or heart attack strikes. So it's very important to have your blood pressure checked periodically.

THE GOOD NEWS

Most high blood pressure responds rapidly to NEWSTART measures, because the low-fat diet, exercise, and hydrotherapy work together to improve circulation of the blood, and the low salt intake helps pull out retained fluid.

Weight loss is very important also, because most blood pressures respond quickly to the loss of even a few pounds. Often, normalizing weight is all that is needed to return a blood pressure to normal range.

Most hypertensives are sensitive to salt and receive considerable benefit from restricting salt intake.

WHAT ABOUT MEDICATION?

There are many medicines that will *control* blood pressure without the need for weight loss, exercising, low-fat diet, and salt restriction. But these medications do not *cure* high blood pressure, and they can have uncomfortable side effects, as you will see in the stories that follow. Medications are expensive and often need to be taken for life. Also, how safe can it be to lower blood pressure with medications, while ignoring the lifestyle factors that promoted it in the first place?

STORY 1:

The Pill Race

My business is real estate, but my passion is sports car racing," Jim told me. "At one time I was one of the top drivers in my class, competing with people like Paul Newman. I won numerous U.S. championships over the years. Then at age 35 I was diagnosed as having serious hypertension." His voice choked on that last word, and he looked away.

Jim was an impressive man, tall, solidly built, and good-looking. His ready smile and easy manner belied the pain I saw in his eyes. "Did that put an end to your racing career?" I thought I knew the answer, but he needed time to compose himself.

"Not exactly," he said, with a hint of a smile. "It just started me on a different kind of race—a pill race—to get my blood pressure down. I began with Dyazide, a diuretic. I followed my doctor's orders, but two things happened: my blood pressure stayed up, and I began getting weaker and weaker. At the time I was competing hard for points in a four-state, divisional championship. Even the short, intense, 45-minute sprint races exhausted me. At the end of one race I collapsed in a heap beside my car and stayed there for 30 minutes, totally drained, trying to get my strength back. I was frightened. Nothing like this had ever happened to me before. I finally got up, but I lost the overall championship by one point."

"And you believe it was because of the Dyazide?"

84

The Lowdown on High Blood Pressure

"I know it was, because it was later discovered that the drug caused me to lose too much potassium, despite my taking potassium supplements. But even after that problem was solved, I didn't feel well. I just wasn't myself. I retired from car racing at the end of the year, but I didn't retire from the pill race."

"What other medications have you taken?" Too few people know what drugs they are taking or understand what the medications are supposed to do. But Jim was different.

"During the next 13 years I took 13 different medicines. After Dyazide there was Ismelin, then Aldomet, Aldoril, Apresoline, Lasix, Inderal, Lopressor, Tenormin, Corgard, Trandate, Minipress, and finally Serax—to calm my stress and anxiety. Unfortunately, each pill gave me a different batch of unpleasant side effects. I endured mental depression, weakness, lassitude, drowsiness, emotional instability, headaches, dizziness, bloating, indigestion, sweating, slurred speech, and worst of all, impotence!"

"You couldn't tolerate any of those medicines? That's quite unusual."

"I know, and some of the doctors told me the reactions were in my head. Those were the most horrible years of my life. I struggled to keep working, hoping things would get better. I was in my prime years with a great many plans for my life. I managed to put together a 500-unit apartment complex, the largest in the county, but physically I kept going down. My doctors continued to switch medications, endeavoring to find one I could tolerate, but I felt worse and worse. Last summer a serious medication reaction caused my blood pressure to soar to 260/140 and landed me in the hospital for two and a half weeks. The doctors at Stanford University diagnosed my problem as hypertension caused by extreme stress. This was hard to understand, because I loved my work and had the best job of my life. I felt my stress came from fighting the side effects of my medications!"

"Then what happened?" I was really into his story by now.

"Basically, I gave up. I left home and my job and moved to a quiet little town in the Sierras. There I met the first doctor who didn't try to 'pill me to death.' He talked to me about lifestyle changes and suggested I go to either Pritikin Longevity Center or Weimar's NEWSTART program. After investigating both, I chose NEWSTART. It was more strict, was within my reach financially, and had a spiritual base—a need I'd felt for some time."

On day one of Jim's NEWSTART program he weighed 223

85

pounds, his blood pressure measured 180/120, and his cholesterol 238 mg/% [6.2 mmol/l]. By the end of the third week he'd dropped 10 pounds, his blood pressure was steady at 135/95, his cholesterol was down to 170 mg/% [4.4 mmol/l], and all medications were gone, except for a small dose of Serax. The last time I saw him, he was exuberant. "The best part is that I feel *good!* My energy level is high, not only in the morning, but throughout the day, without the ups and downs. I can walk five to six miles through the Sierra Nevada foothills without feeling tired. And I've gained a new peace by deepening my spiritual perspectives."

Jim turned philosophical as he reflected on his experience. "It amazes me that the principles that worked to heal me are so simple: wholesome food, physical exercise, adequate water, fresh air and sunshine, temperance in all areas of life, proper rest, and learning to trust one's God.

"These things are available to nearly everyone," he continued, "but sadly, most people don't want to face reality until they find themselves in desperate circumstances. I guess I was pretty desperate when I came here, but I'm young enough to enjoy the quality life I've discovered for a good long time to come. And another thing—now that I've learned how to win the pill race, I'm going back after that checkered flag!"

I phoned him a year later. He was still exuberant and in good health—and was racing again.

STORY 2:

I Blacked Out

Stephan Darden had been my favorite boyfriend in high school. He was lean, lithe, and handsome, with dark wavy hair and a smile that nearly charmed my glasses off. But college had separated us, and we lost track of each other.

Forty years later he arrived on campus for a NEWSTART session. A poignant anticipation surged through me as I ran to meet him. Would I recognize him?

I didn't. My emotions became a brew of surprise, shock, and pain. The beautiful hair had nearly disappeared, and his lithe body was now the shape of a ripe mango. The extra weight puffed his face, erasing the familiar features. But his weary eyes brightened when he saw me, and the voice was the same.

"What has happened to you, dear Stephan?" I asked him. "You look like you've been airlifted out of a battlefield."

"I'll admit I'm scared. I'm finally facing up to how sick I really am. My wife had brain surgery, and I've been so involved in getting her through the crisis and into rehabilitation that I've seriously neglected my own health. I guess I look the way I feel. I'm tired, depressed, defeated. What can you do here for people like me?"

"We specialize in people like you," I said lightly, with a little laugh. "But I'm puzzled about one thing. You state on your chart that you came here to lose 40 pounds. Is weight your only concern? Do you think you can melt off 40 pounds in three weeks? Why do you want to lose 40 pounds, anyway?"

He had to smile at how ridiculous his expectations sounded when I read them back to him. "OK, OK," he said, brightening a bit. "I'll get serious about my problems. I'm overweight, diabetic, hypertensive, and have gout and angina." He looked to see if that was enough to impress me.

"Is that all?" I teased. "Those sound like chronic problems. What *really* brought you here?"

He looked incredulous. "Are you a mind reader or something?" He smiled again at my persistence. "Yes, something did happen that got my attention. One night I was relaxing with the evening paper. As I got up to go to the bedroom, I blacked out. My family found me two hours later, still crumpled on the floor. They summoned the medics. My blood pressure was 210/160. I regained consciousness on the way to the hospital.

"At the emergency room my blood pressure was somewhat better, and there was no sign of a stroke or other catastrophe. I was given several medications and told to go home and take it easy for a few days . . . and to lose some weight.

"I went home and laid around for a few days. I didn't know what to do with myself. I felt bored and ate even more than usual. I realized I wasn't getting better. In fact, I felt so lousy that it scared me into coming here. Now are you happy?" He winked at me, a familiar gesture from the past. Yes, inside was the same funny, wonderful man I'd known before.

"Almost," I said. "But I don't think this happened overnight. The Stephan I knew was one of the healthiest guys on campus."

"I see you're not going to quit until you get my whole life story," he quipped, sighing deeply with feigned weariness.

"Yes, in college I was slender, athletic, and in top health." He spoke with exaggerated patience. "Even after going into the business world, I took special precautions with my health. Until five years ago, I worked out regularly at the YMCA. Even though my weight was inching upward, I remained solidly muscular.

"About that time events piled up on me. My wife became critically ill, needing round-the-clock care. My work involved increasing amounts of travel. My business success involved me in more and more entertaining. Some days I not only had business dinners, but business lunches and even business breakfasts. I knew I was eating too much rich food and exercising too little, but there seemed no way out. Besides, I was feeling OK.

"Then two years ago a painful attack of gout took me to the doctor. He warned me that I would soon have serious health problems if I didn't lose weight and find a way to reduce the stress in my life. My blood pressure was already on the way up, and I was given hypertensive medications.

"I realize now this experience was a wake-up call. It should have scared me into making some serious changes in my life. But at the time I had many pressing matters to attend to. Besides my wife's illness, I had important business appointments waiting, several trips lined up—there seemed to be simply no way to get out of these obligations.

"I am a chemical engineer, specializing in the designing of chemical process plants for handling plastics. I travel all over the country—and much of the world—demonstrating and selling these processes and techniques. It's taken many years to build this successful business, and I wasn't about to let it fall apart. I took off a few days, lost a few pounds, and plunged back into my nonstop life. A few months ago I began feeling increasingly fatigued. My efficiency at work fell markedly. My head seemed full of cobwebs. As my work deteriorated, cold fear edged into my consciousness. I blamed my problems on my medications and stopped taking them. Two months later is when I blacked out. So here I am. What comes next?"

"No," he laughed, "I didn't lose 40 pounds; that was unrealistic. But I did lose 15 pounds, and I've learned how to work off the rest of my weight without starving. And so many other good things have happened. My fasting blood sugar is normal now. My blood pressure is down where it should be, despite a reduction of medication. My cholesterol has dropped to safe levels, and I'm walking six to eight miles a day without needing nitroglycerin.

"But better yet, I've had time to reevaluate my life and obtain new perspectives. I realize this is the kind of lifestyle God intended for us—not only to heal us, but to prevent these kinds of diseases in the first place. A few nights ago I totally rededicated my life to the Lord. I'm beginning to understand what is truly important in my life.

"I deeply appreciate my time here. I couldn't have done this at home. It's not just a better way of exercising and eating, it's a total thing. I needed everything you have here—the loving care, attention, support, and prayers. I needed the group experience, the sharing of problems with other patients, and watching them get well. I needed scientific knowledge that is practical and understandable. Most of all, I needed the experience of actually living the new lifestyle long enough to feel the difference it makes.

> **I realize this is the kind of lifestyle God intended for us—not only to heal us, but to prevent these kinds of diseases in the first place.**

"I can honestly say I'm a renewed man—physically, mentally, emotionally, and spiritually."

Difficult years followed for Stephan. His wife's health deteriorated until she became an invalid. He retired from his business and moved to balmy southern California to devote himself to her care. I saw him from time to time, realizing each time that his life was a constant struggle.

In a May 1996 phone conversation he told me, "Elsie died two years ago. I'm now married to Elizabeth, who was a teacher of nursing for many years. I have lost nearly 70 pounds and feel better than I have in years. Yes, I feel like I'm 40 years old again! And I've gone back to work as a chemical engineer and marketing manager in Grand Rapids, Michigan."

Stephan Darden's NEWSTART experience was 14 years ago. I'd love to see him again.

Feeling Fit

STORY 3:

Set in Concrete

You know how Ben's (not his real name) belly hangs out over his belt? Well, it's getting worse!"

That piece of conversation might have been a laugh line, except that Pat was talking about her husband, and this was not a good omen.

"Is his blood pressure up again?" I wasn't Ben's doctor, but Pat was one of my best friends.

"Probably is, but he hasn't let me check it since he quit his medication." Worry lines creased Pat's face. "The pills make him feel so tired he says he can't stand it. His doctor has tried several different kinds, but they all make him feel tired."

Ben, an electrician and part-time contractor, was active and energetic. He usually worked at least two jobs at a time.

"And I venture to guess he's also sick and tired of hearing about his weight." I knew that Pat cooked healthful food for her family, but Ben was strictly a meat and potatoes man. With lots of gravy. He wouldn't touch anything else except peas and an occasional salad.

"Things changed for a while last Christmas," Pat continued. "Remember when Ben went to buy a new suit, and the salesclerk brought him a portly size? He was so mad he stomped out of the store." Pat smiled at the memory.

"At least it got him back on his diet. I remember he'd lost 20 pounds by Easter, and he looked and felt good. What happened?"

"The same old story. He just won't eat the right kind of food, so he's constantly starving. When he can't stand it any longer, he binges. Look at him now—he's bigger than ever."

I could feel Pat's frustration. This was an ongoing problem that never seemed to get solved. Pat was teary-eyed. "Ben knows he's eating himself into an early grave, and he hates himself for his weakness. But somewhere early in life his dietary habits got set in concrete."

I wanted to encourage her. "At least he doesn't smoke or drink. And his work gives him plenty of outdoor exercise. He has those things in his favor."

"He must have a pretty strong heart, too," Pat added. "At least he's never had angina."

Sadly, Ben had a sudden massive heart attack at age 55. He wasn't expected to live, but he survived. For a year he sat at home, tethered to an oxygen tank. He sometimes puttered around in his toolshed.

When Ben got stronger, he and Pat packed up their Airstream trailer and joined a group of volunteer church builders. Ben could at least supervise some of the electrical work. "I haven't gone to a foreign field," he'd tell his friends, "but I feel like a missionary."

Ben continued to help in this way until a second heart attack ended his life at age 59. His widow and children carry on. And yes, his diet remained set in concrete to the end.

STORY 4:

The Robot Awakens

I've been walking around in a daze, feeling like a robot, for nearly two years," Jean said. "I can't take it anymore. I've gotten so depressed I hardly care to live." Her tired, listless eyes contrasted sharply with her attractive, youthful appearance and her stylish clothes. I probed to discover her problem.

"I was pretty much OK until two years ago. I began feeling stressed and tired and had trouble sleeping, so I went for a physical checkup. The doctor diagnosed high blood pressure and started me on medications. I'm now taking eight different kinds."

"For your blood pressure?"

"Let's see, I think three are for my blood pressure, one is to calm my nerves, and two others help me sleep—" She stopped, suddenly self-conscious, and shifted her focus. "Nothing helped; in fact, I felt worse. Finally I got so upset I threw them all out and quit, cold turkey. But my blood pressure went up again, and the doctor told me sternly that those medications must be taken for life, and I had better make up my mind to it.

"I feel trapped in a life I hate, but I see no way out." Her eyes were pleading now. "I have a wonderful husband, but I'm no longer an adequate wife." She looked away, blinking hard.

"Look at me, Jean," I commanded. I took her hands in mine. "God sent you here, and we can help you!"

A small smile began to tug at her face. "Actually, my uncle sent me here," she corrected. "But I know I'm grasping at a straw, and I'm scared to death. I guess I do need God." She sat on the edge of her chair, opening and closing her hands as we began talking about her treatment.

"Jean, do you realize the length of your depression coincides almost exactly with the length of time you've been on heavy medication? How do you feel about slowly cutting down the dosages while you are here?"

Jean froze, panic and terror in her eyes. She was right. She was scared to death. She truly believed that her very survival depended on those medications.

I backed off. "OK, let's compromise. You pick out one medicine, and we'll reduce the dose just a little bit. We'll watch you carefully, monitor your blood pressure, and restore the dose if anything happens."

Jean gradually settled into the program. She was introduced to low-fat, low-salt, high-fiber food, and to miles of beautiful trails on which to walk. She learned how to lose weight and enjoyed the hydrotherapy treatments and the sunbaths. She drank gallons of water. Day by day her confidence increased and her medication doses shrank. She walked between five and six

Jean froze, panic and terror in her eyes. She was scared to death. She truly believed that her very survival depended on those medications.

miles a day and lost 13 pounds. Her blood cholesterol dropped an astounding 93 mg/% [2.4 mmol/l], from 278 mg/% [7.1 mmol/l] to 185 mg/% [4.8 mmol/l]. By the last 10 days of the program she was off all medications, and her blood pressure remained right around 120/80. Jean purchased her own blood pressure equipment so she could check it herself.

Wondering what was going on, Jean's husband flew down from Canada to check things out. He was trim, fit, friendly, and very handsome—every bit the prize Jean had described.

"I can't believe what I'm seeing!" he exclaimed. "Is this vital, alert, gorgeous woman really my wife?"

"You bet I am!" Jean shot back, as they hugged each other. "The robot woke up and walked back into reality. Come on, I'll race you to the cemetery!"

The final week of Jean's 25-day stay was a honeymoon special for two excited people. They hiked the trails, hand in hand, sweethearts once more.

"We have a lot of lost time to make up for," Mr. Wonderful told me with a wink.

A few years later I met Jean and her husband at camp meeting in Alberta.

"When we left Weimar, we felt God had definitely been leading us," they told me. "We took Bible studies and were baptized two years ago."

During my health presentation that afternoon, Jean was Exhibit A. Her radiant health and obvious joy made her testimony more effective than anything I could say about the value of the Adventist lifestyle and the rewards of taking it seriously.

Author's Note: Not everyone responds as dramatically as Jean did. Not everyone with high blood pressure can get off medication. On the other hand, the majority of hypertensives can get off medication—or at least reduce their dosages—by paying attention to lifestyle factors. Medications have their place, but should generally be a last resort. The side effects of Jean's medications nearly ruined her life.

STORY 5:

Backing Out of Kidney Failure

We didn't know Carol's grandfather was in kidney failure when he arrived at our health center. Carol, our head nurse, had brought him to NEWSTART for help with his hypertension. Her grandfather was E. L. Minchin, who had been a powerful youth leader in the Adventist denomination during most of my lifetime. His erect form, ruggedly handsome features, and dignified manner radiated strength, even at age 77. I would have been thoroughly intimidated except for his face. His blue eyes twinkled with good humor, and the warmth of his smile could melt ice cubes in the fridge.

He felt a little dizzy when he arrived, so Carol took his blood pressure. It was so low we warned him not to take his medications the next morning. Elder Minchin (none of us could call him Len) told us he'd been taking large doses of potent medicine for five months with minimal effect on his blood pressure. The medicine upset his stomach and made him tired and irritable.

He had expected his blood pressure to improve so the medicine could be decreased, but this didn't happen.

"You have a serious, intractable [resistant to treatment] case of hypertension," the doctor had said. "You'll probably have to continue the medicines for the rest of your life."

We explained that the relaxation of his leisurely week of travel had potentiated the effects of his medications, and that his blood pressure would probably start going up again. This happened, but during the next 25 days it didn't go high enough to resume medication.

Elder Minchin's blood pressure became a secondary concern when we looked at his laboratory results. His blood urea nitrogen (BUN) was much too high, and what was worse, the creatinine was elevated. An elevated BUN could often be reversed, but an elevated creatinine usually indicated serious kidney failure. Since he was neither diabetic nor dehydrated, we asked him about previous kidney disease.

"About 11 years ago I was quite ill for several weeks, and the doctors said that disease damaged my kidneys. From that time on I had 'spells' of hypertension, caused by my chronic kidney disease, they said. I could usually control these spells by a change of pace—cutting down on stress and pressure and occasionally with medication. It seemed to me that when my kidneys were working well, my blood pressure would improve."

His diagnosis was right on, we told him. When kidneys fall behind in their ability to clear wastes from the blood, they often secrete a substance that raises the blood pressure. This temporarily helps the kidneys by improving circulation. But a raised blood pressure, in time, will also increase kidney damage.

Elder Minchin was quiet for a few moments, then spoke in a voice betraying his concern. "Now that my blood pressure . . . won't come down . . . does that mean . . . my kidneys are too damaged to recover?"

"Your kidneys are working," we assured him. "It's likely they are just overloaded. Kidneys have a great reserve. Do you know that people can live with as little as 10 percent of kidney function?"

"Do you think mine are that far gone?" Shreds of hope mingled with his concern.

We told him we didn't know, at this point. But we assured him we would teach him how to help his kidneys get rid of the overload and how to protect them from further damage. Here was the plan:

- Drink lots of water. Damaged kidneys don't concentrate wastes very well, so extra water is needed to wash them out.
- Drastically limit salt intake. Salt, combined with poor kidney function, promotes fluid retention, another cause of hypertension.
- It's important to eat a low-fat diet. The kidneys must help detoxify and eliminate the ketones and certain other products of fat metabolism. By lowering fat intake, one also decreases the load on the kidneys.
- And it is very important to eat a very low-protein diet. Contrary to common belief, adults require little protein, because their bodies are able to recycle most of what they need. The metabolism of excess amounts of protein forms urea nitrogen and other toxic, irritating substances that the kidneys must detoxify and eliminate. These substances act as diuretics, which means that the kidneys use extra amounts of water to flush them out. Healthy kidneys manage to handle the excessive amounts of protein most Westerners eat, but damaged kidneys are another story.

> I'm 77 years old, and I suppose I shouldn't expect to feel young indefinitely, but it's certainly a relief to know that some of the old feelings are still there.

"Let me see," Elder Minchin broke in. "That leaves the carbohydrates. What effect do they have on the kidneys?"

"The good news is that fruit and starches do not stress kidneys. Carbohydrates supply the energy the body needs—much like gasoline does to a car. But unlike gasoline, carbohydrates burn clean, the end products being water, which goes out of the kidney unchanged, and carbon dioxide, which is eliminated each time we exhale. Since your weight is normal, you can stuff yourself with all the carbohydrate foods your heart desires."

"Good news. Is that all?"

"Not quite. Daily exercise is next on the list. Walk several miles each day. Soon your kidneys will be getting more fresh, oxygenated blood than they've seen for quite a while."

Elder Minchin's face looked like daybreak. "This is absolutely fascinating!" he said. "And everything you've mentioned, I can do."

And that was exactly what he did do for the next 25 days. His BUN returned to normal, and best of all, his blood creatinine came down. (At that time it was believed that once the creatinine began to rise, it was usually not possible to lower it, short of kidney dialysis.)

"It scares me to think that I almost didn't come here," he told me one day as we hiked the Manzanita Trail. "I just couldn't see what good it would do. I was a lifelong vegetarian and lived a healthy life. When needed, I consistently sought the finest available medical help. What more could be done? Besides, I was already booked into a busy summer camp meeting schedule."

"So how did Carol manage to get you here?"

"Well, my depression got worse, and my stomach was so irritated I no longer enjoyed my meals. My reluctance finally gave way, and I was ready for an infusion of hope. I canceled the camp meeting schedule and called Carol to reserve a place for me. It's hard to believe how much has changed in such a short time," he continued. "My depression lifted in a week. My energy is returning—my old 'oomph' that I feared was gone forever. I'm 77 years old, and I suppose I shouldn't expect to feel young indefinitely, but it's certainly a relief to know that some of the old feelings are still there."

As we were all saying goodbye, Elder Minchin made a confession. "When I came here, I thought *you* people were the fanatics. But it's the other way around. *I* am now the fanatic. I have to be. To stay well, to keep my damaged kidneys functioning, to keep my blood pressure down, from now on I will be the strictest of the strict—an extremist, if you please! But it's worth it. My life has been given back to me."

But he couldn't stay serious for long. "Oh, one other thing." His eyes narrowed into a mischievous glimmer. "I love the way you doctors chop wood and work in the garden with us. And I love the way you take turns doing dishes in the cafeteria!"

Elder Minchin lived six more years after his NEWSTART experience.

"If this doesn't open them up, it's diet
and exercise for you!"

Coronary Heart Disease:

A Word From the Pioneers

*Heart disease before age 80 is our fault—not God's fault,
or nature's will.*—Paul Dudley White, M.D.,
President Eisenhower's physician

Dr. Dean Ornish presented the first solid scientific evidence that it is actually possible to reverse heart disease without drugs or surgery. The following are excerpts from his book, *Dr. Dean Ornish's Program for Reversing Heart Disease.*

• More men and women die from coronary artery disease each year than from all other causes of death combined, including cancer and AIDS.

• We have gotten to a point in medicine where it is somehow considered radical, or an ordeal, to ask people to stop smoking, manage stress better, walk, and eat a healthful diet. And it is considered conservative to saw people open and bypass the arteries, or to slip balloons inside the arteries and squish them, or put them on powerful drugs for the rest of their lives. I think our medical priorities are a little topsy-turvy.

• The Reversal Diet is a very low-fat, vegetarian diet that contains no animal products, except egg whites and nonfat dairy. This is what was consumed by patients in our study whose coronary heart disease began to reverse. I am convinced that this is the world's healthiest diet for most adults, whether or not they have heart disease.

• [This program] is about how to enjoy living, not how to avoid dying; how to manage stress, not how to avoid it; how to live in the world more fully, not how to withdraw from it; how to take care of yourself so that you can give more fully to others.

• When people learn to experience inner peace, then they are more likely to make and maintain lifestyle choices that are life-enhancing, rather than self-destructive.

Feeling Fit

Every two years for the past 48 years, the health of 5,000 residents of one Massachusetts town has been carefully studied and documented by the famous Framingham Heart Study, of which Dr. William Castelli is director. This study has become the most valuable scientific resource available in assessing the risk factors of heart disease.

Dr. Castelli, now 66 years old, is the first man among his kin to turn 50 without suffering a heart attack. "I'm living proof that you can beat the odds of heart disease, even if it runs in your family," he says.

While Dr. Castelli was still in his 30s, he began to notice that people who had high cholesterol had the most heart attacks. His own cholesterol was 270 mg/% [7.0 mmol/l]. "That's when the light went on," he says.

He started jogging every day and cut down on his dietary fat. He brought his cholesterol down to 190 mg/% [4.9 mmol/l] and his HDL (good cholesterol) from 49 (1.5) to a healthier 63 (4.2). He insists that a healthy lifestyle doesn't have to take the pleasure out of life. A person can significantly decrease the odds of having a heart attack by simply substituting low-fat foods for high-fat ones and taking brisk walks several times a week.

Dr. Castelli wants everyone to face the facts of heart disease:

• High total cholesterol and low HDL are among the strongest predictors of heart disease.

• High blood pressure increases the risk of heart attacks and strokes by up to five times.

• Smokers have a 70 percent chance of dying from a heart attack.

"If you want to produce coronary artery disease in monkeys, all you have to do is feed them an average hospital diet," Dr. Castelli says. "But if you want to reverse the coronary artery disease in these monkeys, all you have to do is feed them a simple, low-fat vegetarian diet. The problem in Western society is that you've got to be a monkey to get proper dietary treatment for heart disease."

COMMENTS FROM HERE AND THERE

Close to 90 percent of all coronary deaths could be prevented if the cholesterol was kept below 182 mg percent, the blood pressure under 120 mm Hg, and [there was] no smoking or diabetes.—Professor Jeremiah Stamler, M.D.

A Word from the Pioneers

All the majesty of the mind can be dethroned by the stomach.—U. D. Register, Ph.D.

It's painful to face the truth—that we are really killing ourselves.—Frank Ginsberg.

My doctor told me to cut down on red meat. Since then I have stopped putting ketchup on my hamburgers.—Contributed.

The best doctors in the world are Doctor Diet, Doctor Quiet, and Doctor Merryman.—Jonathan Swift, 1738.

Consciously or unconsciously, most people make sacrifices of some sort. Unfortunately, they often sacrifice health, family, religion, or other priceless possessions in order to gain the transitory pleasures of wealth, status, or fame.—Contributed.

STORY 1:

Outwitting Sudden Death

Beverly was alone when the pain hit, right between her shoulder blades. She was watching the last few minutes of a television program before turning in for the night. Her husband, Bud, had flown to Sacramento that morning.

She sat very still. The pain worsened and began boring through her chest. She felt nauseated. The dire prediction of her cardiologist flashed into her mind: "If you have a heart attack, you won't have any warning," he had said, looking at her angiogram. "Your first symptom will be sudden death." He showed Beverly where her left anterior descending coronary artery was 75 percent blocked, up near its beginning. "If blood supplies are shut off at that point, there won't be enough heart left to keep you alive."

Beverly took a deep breath and looked around. She pinched herself. "But I am alive," she concluded.

She reached for the phone to call 911, then paused. *Screaming ambulances. People rushing around. Needles, oxygen masks, monitors, loud voices, curious neighbors.* "No," she decided. "I can't handle that." She got into her car and headed for the Eisenhower Medical Center. She walked calmly into the bedlam of the emergency room, looking perfectly fine and feeling ridiculous. With accident victims all around her, she almost fled to her car and drove home. But the worsening pain stopped her. So she wrote a note:

101

Feeling Fit

I think I may be having a heart attack, but I'm not sure. My left coronary artery was 75 percent blocked four years ago. My cholesterol is over 300 mg/% [7.8 mmol/l].

Within minutes she was whisked into an examining room and given a nitroglycerin tablet. The pain stopped, and she was admitted to coronary intensive care. Around midnight Dr. Benson appeared, introducing himself as a cardiologist. He suspected a heart attack, he said, but it would be several hours before he could be sure.

Curled up in her crisp white hospital bed, wide awake now, Beverly began thinking about her mother and grandmother. Both had died in their 40s of coronary heart disease. Yet for most of her life Beverly had floated along, blissfully denying that their problem related to her.

Seven years before, she finally woke up. Flat in bed with a back injury, she faced the reality of her declining health. Her hypertension wasn't responding to medication, her cholesterol was 350 mg/% [8.3 mmol/l], and she was 30 pounds overweight. Her back hurt, and her energy and zest for life were fading. These were the same symptoms her mother and grandmother had had.

> **Beverly began thinking about her mother and grandmother. Both had died in their 40s of coronary heart disease.**

Beverly found a health center nearby with a live-in program that emphasized natural remedies as a primary means of restoring health. Having worked for years in doctors' offices, she was eager to explore alternative therapies.

For 25 days she listened, watched, studied, and participated with unbelieveable results. Her blood pressure came down, pounds seem to melt off, and her cholesterol dropped more than 100 points [2.6 mmol/l]. She was able to stop all her medications. She felt so good, she determined to follow these health concepts to the letter for the rest of her life. The next two years were among the best of her life. She was healthy, happy, fit, played golf every day, and shared her experiences with anyone who would listen.

Then a crisis intervened. Her daughter became critically ill. For weeks Beverly existed in motels under makeshift conditions to be near as her daughter fought for her life. Engulfed in anxiety and disruption, Beverly stopped thinking about her own health. Even when the crisis passed, she was too emotionally spent to care. Two years went by.

Then a swing at a golf ball, a searing pain, and it was as if she'd hit the rerun button of her life—back pain, overweight, hypertension, and sky-high cholesterol. It wasn't easy to return to the NEWSTART Health Center, but she did it. Once more she worked to regain her health, and once more she went home renewed and motivated. This time she followed the advice of her NEWSTART doctor and went to see a cardiologist. Her angiogram revealed serious blockage. She was advised to take cholesterol-lowering drugs. She thought about the many side effects and complications she would have to deal with, not to mention the unending laboratory tests and doctor's visits. Then she thought about the wonderful results she'd had with diet and right living and chose to give NEWSTART another try.

In time Beverly and Bud moved to a country club home in Palm Springs, California. Surrounded by luxury and people who were busily soaking up their version of "the good life," the couple felt themselves slipping.

About this time they met some members of the "Lopers," a popular running club in Loma Linda. Members met weekly to train for different kinds of events. The one that excited Beverly and Bud the most was the Honolulu Marathon, 11 months away. They both joined the club, even though it meant a 120-mile round trip each week from Palm Springs. Lean, athletic Bud trained for serious competition, but Beverly stuck to brisk walking. Within six months she could do nine or ten miles at a stretch and felt good. No clouds on her horizon!

Beverly's reverie ended abruptly as Dr. Benson bustled in with a handful of records. "Thanks to fax, here are copies of your angiogram and records from up north." The doctor studied her quizzically. "With this much heart disease, would you tell me why you haven't seen a doctor for nearly three years?"

Beverly liked this man and gave it to him straight. "Because I can't find one who will take me seriously. They laugh at exercise and diet as treatments. They are determined to load me up with pills."

The doctor laughed good-naturedly. Then he told her she hadn't had a heart attack—she had passed a gallstone! She needed gallbladder surgery. "But before a surgeon will touch you, you'll have to have an angiogram and a stress electro-cardiogram."

Bud was with Beverly for her angiogram the next day. As he finished, Dr. Benson jumped up. "Look at this! Your obstruction is now only 60 percent. Your blockage is reversing!"

The following Monday Beverly mounted the treadmill for the stress test. "Are you OK? Are you sure you want to go on?" she was asked each time the the incline was made steeper or the speed was increased. Well into stage 3 they stopped the test.

"No, no, let's go some more," Beverly urged.

"I can't believe this," said the doctor.

The gallbladder surgery was a breeze, and Beverly went home a day early, mostly to get some good food. "Another day of hospital specials and I'd have had a heart attack for sure!" she said.

"Bud and I are 'riding high in the saddle' again," she reports. "We are eating at least 80 percent perfectly, and we have an abundance of new, health-minded friends. We love our excursions with the Lopers. We'll be in Hawaii next month, where I'll be doing the minimarathon. But watch out for Bud—he's planning to win!"

"Oh, yes," she added, "my wonderful new cardiologist delivered his verdict: no pills. 'Just keep on doing whatever it is you are doing.'"

BEVERLY'S STRATEGY

People often ask Beverly how she does it. Here, briefly, is her formula:

1. No "quickie diets." Go for the long term.

2. Focus on healthy food: plenty of high fiber, unrefined foods (plant foods), and a minimum of high-fat, fiberless foods (meat, eggs, dairy).

3. Make exercise a priority: one hour a day for weight loss, and at least half an hour for maintenance.

4. Drinking water liberally before and between meals decreases the need for snacks and beverages.

5. Avoid all harmful substances.

6. Great stress reducers include sunshine, fresh air, adequate rest, and trust in divine power.

"I'm certainly not perfect. My NEWSTART experience has been like riding a bicycle. You fall off, you get back on, but you never forget how to ride," Beverly says. "Unfortunately, I do fall off that bicycle every now and again, but right now I'm back on the program and loving every minute of it. It's amazing what it does for my psyche. I'm 68 years old now and still going strong."

A Word From the Pioneers

STORY 2:

Slow but Sure

When Hank arrived at the NEWSTART lodge, he couldn't get out of bed and go to the bathroom without pain. A recent angiogram had demonstrated such extensive heart disease that bypass or other surgical procedures were out of the question. "Hank," his doctor had said, "medically, there just isn't any more we can do for you. I'm sorry."

His daughter had heard about the NEWSTART program and urged him to go. He wondered if it would do any good, if the expense would be justified. After all, he was at the end of the medical rope. That night he had an attack of angina pain so severe that he decided to go. "If there is any chance I can be helped, it had better be now," he told his wife.

During the first week of Hank's program he could do little more than walk to the cafeteria and to physical therapy. But the night pain was gradually lessening, and by the end of the second week he could walk a half mile without pain. Hank was delighted, but curious. "Why am I getting better so soon?" he asked the doctors. "There hasn't been time for collateral circulation or plaque reversal to occur." (Hank had learned these terms from the medical lectures.)

> **People don't realize that when they eat a high-fat diet, the excess fat thickens their blood, and circulation becomes sluggish.**

"That's a very good question," the doctors told him. "People don't realize that when they eat a high-fat diet, the excess fat thickens their blood, and circulation becomes sluggish. It's possible to observe this milky-looking blood in the small vessels of the human eye or in a rabbit's ear. Another thing that happens is what we call rouleau formation. Fat-thickened blood is sticky, causing red blood cells to adhere to each other in bunches. These clumped blood cells cannot carry their full load of oxygen, and they are unable to navigate tiny capillaries."

"You mean this no-fat diet I'm eating is cleaning out my blood?" Hank was incredulous.

"You are actually eating a low-fat diet—in your case very low, about 10 percent of your daily calories. Because this fat occurs naturally in your food, you don't see it."

"So you can actually slip more oxygen to my heart muscle by thinning out my blood!" Hank exclaimed.

"That's the idea. Every little bit of extra oxygen that reaches your heart helps it grow stronger and decreases the pain of angina."

"And it's possible for me to get better slowly." Hank was trying to absorb the concept. "This is wonderful news! I'm going over to the cafeteria to apologize for my complaints about the food."

Hank continued to improve gradually. After three weeks he could walk two miles a day, slowly, but without pain. Because of his precarious situation, Hank decided to stay another month. His endurance continued to improve, and at the end of the second month he could walk a little more than four miles a day without pain. He didn't do this all at one time, but in bits and pieces throughout the day.

When Hank left for home, he carried his own suitcases to the car. He reports he can now work nearly all day. He goes slowly, taking up to a week sometimes to accomplish what he could once do in a day. "But I'm doing it without pain, as long as I pace myself. I have a long way to go yet, but little by little my endurance is increasing. I feel my recovery is a direct blessing from God, and I thank Him daily. I'd like to share my experience with others who might feel that the way is too hard or that recovery is too slow. Stick with it. Life is worth it."

STORY 3:

The Textbook Case

It's hard to accept that I have advanced heart disease at 42 years of age," Dennis Hale told us. "I ski during the winter and go whitewater canoeing and backpacking the rest of the time. I belong to a mountain rescue team and was out on a strenuous mission only four months ago. Now I can't walk 100 feet up my driveway without extreme, shattering pain." Tall,

A Word From the Pioneers

athletic, and tan, Dennis certainly looked the picture of health. He wasn't carrying an extra pound on his muscular frame.

"The worst part is that my two boys are just getting old enough to go with me on these excursions. We recently finished outfitting ourselves with all the gear we need." Dennis looked at the floor, swallowing hard. "I guess that part of my life is over. I'll have to develop some quieter hobbies."

He didn't have a great deal of optimism when he came down from Canada to join a NEWSTART program. The year was 1980, and few people believed then that those hard plaques obstructing the coronary arteries could be reversed, and almost nobody worried about cholesterol levels. According to conventional wisdom it was something a person was born with, and it rarely changed.

Dennis quickly grasped the NEWSTART concepts. Despite the lack of scientific proof at that time, the NEWSTART physicians believed that given a very low-fat diet of about 10 percent of calories as fat, along with other positive lifestyle factors, a person could, over a period of time, regain a portion of the cardiac strength that had been lost. Whether it was reversal, collateral circulation, or something else, they weren't sure, but they had seen it happen a number of times.

I was new on the staff at the time, and Dennis was the first person I had a chance to know well and to follow over a period of time. He spent 25 days with the NEWSTART program and left feeling greatly encouraged and full of hope.

"I've decided not to sell our outdoor sports equipment," he announced with a big smile.

We didn't hear from Dennis for two years, but then he sent us a comprehensive report that sounded almost like a case report in a textbook.

In 1981, one year after my NEWSTART experience, I participated in a 25-kilometer ski race, pacing myself on the edge of pain. I also went cross-country skiing, but now and then my buddies had to wait for me.

In 1982, two years after NEWSTART, I again joined a 25-kilometer ski race. This time I went as fast as my old body would allow, with slight pain on the uphill part, and no pain the rest of the way. My cross-country skiing buddies no longer had to wait for me. I kept right up with them.

I can now carry a 40-pound pack all day in the roughest of the high country at my old preangina pace. No problem with

107

whitewater canoeing, either, even in the toughest rapids. I can do everything I did before the angina started. The boys are delighted, and so am I.

My doctor, an internist with 20 years of practice experience, does all the treadmill stress tests in this valley. He is astounded by my improvement, saying I was the only angina patient he had ever seen who showed any degree of improvement. He added that my improvement was so considerable that in his opinion I had experienced a fair degree of reversal.

Dennis attached a report of his cholesterol levels, correlated with his diet.

In late 1994 I wrote a letter to Dennis and received the following reply from his wife, Alice:

By 1984 all trace of Dennis's angina was gone. He climbed mountains to his heart's content and won a bronze medal in long-distance skiing that year.

The next few years were good years for the Hale family. Dennis remained healthy and active, feeling no limitations at all. He remained faithful to his NEWSTART diet, following it at least 90 percent.

In 1992 Dennis went on a two-week canoe trip. On that trip a tragic accident took his life.

STORY 4:

The Living Museum

Imagine a museum full of different diseases. That was Art Dryden when he arrived at NEWSTART. At age 46 he'd barely survived a massive heart attack and was given five years to live. A few years later a serious stroke left him badly damaged. Life became a series of leg cramps, angina pains, blackouts, and stomach problems. Finally another heart attack led to bypass surgery, then more surgery to remove blockage from a carotid (neck) artery.

He arrived at NEWSTART in 1984, badly deteriorated. What more could be done? Even optimistic NEWSTART doctors wondered. But tiny sparks of hope flickered in wife Barbara's eyes. Yes, with many prayers we would do what we could. And Art responded. He began to walk again, a little farther each day as the pains eased. His cholesterol dropped 50 mg/% [1.3 mmol/l] and his triglycerides went from 446 mg/% [10.8 mmol/l] to 209 mg/% [5.3 mmol/l]. He kept losing weight and feeling better. His stomach pain disappeared.

Ten years later Barbara sent us the following report: Art lived nine more years after his NEWSTART experience. He lost 20 pounds and kept them off. He got to the point where he could walk several miles a day without pain. "We stuck to the diet until the last two years. Art was 73 by then and decided he'd lived a long and fulfilling life and just wanted to relax and enjoy himself. We began going out to eat more frequently, and he ate what he wanted. He said he was ready to go. Tomorrow was OK, he said. Maybe OK with him, but not with me. We lost him November 10, 1993. We miss him, but we're so thankful he was able to live out his threescore and ten, despite the serious diseases and dire predictions."

STORY 5:

Springing the Heart Trap

You must give up jogging immediately," intoned the doctor solemnly. "You've got a heart problem. Here are some nitroglycerin tablets you can take for pain. We'll schedule an angiogram as soon as we can."

Donald Cox walked out of the office in shocked disbelief. He'd come to the doctor because he had the flu. True, he'd had a few chest pains lately, but he'd blamed it on an upset stomach. "I can't have a heart problem," he sputtered to his wife. "Why, I jog every day, play golf, climb mountains, fly planes—how could I have heart disease?"

However, the angiogram revealed four major blockages in his heart arteries, the most serious one being in the large left descending coronary artery. It was nearly 80 percent obstructed. Donald felt cheated and depressed. He pictured himself fiddling around the house for the rest of his life, a dismal outlook for a man who went regularly on major safaris, collecting animals for various museums.

His family doctor returned with a heart surgeon. "You have serious problems," he said. "If you want to be active at all in the future, or fly again, you must have the operation."

"OK, you say when," he heard himself say.

Surgery was scheduled for the next week. In the meantime Donald and his wife heard about a place out West where some kinds of heart problems were treated with diet and exercise. He called Dr. Art Weaver, a cardiovascular surgeon in Detroit. Dr. Weaver knew about the program and highly recommended it. But he warned Donald that he would need to be on an extremely strict program to get the results he needed. It would take a lot of dedication and motivation to stick with it.

"Let's go," Donald said. "I'll do anything to avoid heart surgery, even if I have to live on grass."

Despite their family doctor's dire prediction that they were wasting not only money but precious time, they joined the 25-day NEWSTART program. Exercise was no problem, as Donald was already walking/jogging 40 miles per week. He gradually increased this to 80 miles per week while at NEWSTART. He was so excited when his chest discomfort (angina) disappeared that we had to remind him he wasn't well yet. It was just that getting the thick, sticky, excess fat out of his blood improved his coronary circulation just enough to allow his heart to keep up with his activities.

> I can't have a heart problem. Why, I jog every day, play golf, climb mountains, fly planes—how could I have heart disease?

The food was another matter. Whenever he felt like complaining, though, he would say "bypass" out loud, and that settled the matter. In time he came to enjoy the simple, natural food. He knew that for him, this very low-fat diet must be followed for the rest of his life. By the time he left NEWSTART, his blood cholesterol had dropped from 222 mg/% [5.7 mmol/l] to a much safer 141 mg/% [3.6 mmol/l].

Once at home, the couple worked hard to duplicate the NEWSTART program. By the end of a year Donald's stress treadmill test showed considerable increase in exercise tolerance, and even more tolerance at the end of the second year.

Early in the third year Donald went back to serious hunting. A safari to Nepal (home of Mount Everest) took him to elevations of 15,000 feet with no problems. Later he climbed the Tibetan Plateau in China, at 16,000 feet elevation. He has continued his hunting trips in the high mountains ever since.

At this writing it's been five years since that day Donald faced bypass surgery. His present cardiologist approves of his lifestyle and encourages him. "Your treadmill stress test is now within normal limits," the doctor said at the five-year mark. "I'm certain you've experienced reversal, although I don't feel you should undergo the risk and expense of another angiogram just to prove it.

"You've made a believer out of me. I'm putting myself on the diet too," the doctor added.

STORY 6:

The Making of a New Connie

Connie Thebarge was told by her physicians at the Ottawa Heart Institute that there was nothing they could do for her that hadn't already been done. She had received a triple coronary bypass and then, four years later, an angioplasty. In addition, she was taking 27 pills a day for her coronary heart disease, gout, hypertension, and depression, and 60 units of insulin for her diabetes. She couldn't walk more than 100 yards without popping nitro pills. She was so depressed that she asked her husband to put her into a nursing home.

Instead, he enrolled her in the Ottawa Coronary Heart Improvement Project (or C.H.I.P., one of Dr. Hans Diehl's community health education seminars). Two years later she is down to three pills a day. Her insulin is at half the level that it was before, and she is walking three miles a day and swimming on a regular basis. Instead of being depressed, she went on a health cruise to Alaska, visited England, and is on her way to Australia. Most of her pain is gone. She has become a new woman. And instead of spending $750 a month for medications, she now has a bill of $80 a month.

Asked how her physician reacted, Connie says, "My doctor was very skeptical at first. His eyes later widened in disbelief, and he began to inquire about the nutritional and lifestyle aspects of the program. Some of my specialists are quite excited and have even referred some of their patients to me, in hopes that I might be able to motivate them and provide some education."

STORY 7:

The Hundred-Mile Wonder

I walked out of that doctor's office determined never to darken his door again." Alice Humphrey spat the words out like they were coals of fire. "He kept switching my medicines around and around, while I continued to go downhill. My feet were so swollen I couldn't walk. I couldn't go to bed; I had to sit up all night to breathe. I had diabetes, hypertension, and serious heart failure. I knew I was dying."

She was telling the truth. I'd first met this tiny spitfire on her third day of the NEWSTART program. She was still sitting up to breathe. I remember wondering who had ever accepted her into our program. We weren't equipped to handle acutely ill patients, and this woman was certainly in advanced heart failure.

It was as if she read my mind. "I'm not sure how I got here myself," she said. "I came from Phoenix, 850 miles away. The doctors here were not overjoyed to see me, but they didn't have the heart to send me home. I told them not to worry—whatever happened to me was all right. I was ready to go. But I felt a lot better being in the hands of Christian doctors who believed in the Adventist lifestyle."

Against all odds, this amazing woman began getting better. The saltless food helped pull the extra water out of her body, and the swelling in her legs went down. Her breathing got easier. She started walking. The unbelievable thing was that by the twenty-fifth day she had walked 100 miles!

I found Alice again two years later. She was in overalls, scraping paint from an old building. She told me she drives the 850 miles from Phoenix to Weimar twice a year: once for the annual two-week work bee, and once for alumni homecoming week. I wanted to know more about what had happened since her NEWSTART experience, and she was eager to tell me.

"My heart failure disappeared and has not recurred. My blood sugar has been normal for two years. I've lost a total of 50 pounds. I take one Lanoxin tablet a day, and one Inderal tablet. That's all.

"I work 10 to 12 hours a day. When I'm not volunteering here or somewhere else, I take in ironing. I exercise regularly and follow the diet strictly and consistently. I'm happy. I feel great. I'm nearly 70 years old and excited about my future.

"It's hard to realize that during the four years before my NEWSTART experience, I was in and out of the hospital nine times. I'd get these attacks of tachycardia [very fast heartbeat], and they would do cardioversion [shock the heart back into a normal rhythm]. I was in the doctor's office at least monthly.

"But no more! No more hospitalizations, no more doctor's office visits, except my NEWSTART doctors. I praise God for what has happened to me."

Almost every time I returned to Weimar over the next several years, I'd meet Alice again, always happy, feeling fine, and always busy helping out. And every time I'd feel the same amazement all over again.

And I too praise God anew for leading me into such a rewarding way to practice medicine.

STORY 8:

I'm the Cook

by Roy Scales (name supplied)

I was in sad shape when I first arrived at NEWSTART 14 years ago. I had seriously plugged coronary arteries, I was overweight, my blood pressure was too high, and I felt generally lousy. I was 66 years old.

My 25 days at NEWSTART improved me markedly and opened my eyes to the possibilities of a new life. The food has been no problem, because I do all the cooking (to my wife's delight). During the past 14 years I have been 90 to 95 percent faithful to the NEWSTART way of eating. I exercise an hour every day and have felt just great.

In 1984 my wife and I enjoyed a wonderful trip through Europe. By planning ahead, we found places to stay where we could do most of our own cooking. Neither my diabetic wife nor I got out of control on the trip. We enjoyed every minute of it.

I felt fine after my 1982 NEWSTART and thanked God I hadn't had to go through bypass surgery.

In late 1993 I was persuaded to have an angiogram. The doctor said I needed some bypasses. I told him I was walking four miles in 60 minutes almost daily, with no problems at all, but he acted unimpressed. He said I had a bad mitral valve, and he would have to fix that.

During the valve surgery he did the bypasses as well, even though I was nearly 80 years old and didn't feel I needed them. I've had nothing but problems since. I'm still unhappy with that doctor!

STORY 9:

Wanda's Mistake

I f I'd known what the NEWSTART program was really like, I would never have come," Wanda told me after we had gotten to know each other. "By the third day I was sure I'd made a terrible mistake."

She could see that I was surprised, but she was smiling, so I knew the situation wasn't too serious.

"My decision to come here was impulsive," she explained. "I was facing my third angiogram, and I not only didn't want it, but dreaded hearing what the doctors would say afterward—that I needed open-heart surgery. Someone told me that going through the NEWSTART program could help people avoid bypass surgery, so I packed up and came."

I was puzzled. "Don't you think the program measures up?"

"Oh, yes, the program lives up to its reputation, but I discovered something else. This is a Christian place. People here believe in God, have faith, pray, sing, and love you earnestly, no matter how obnoxious you are! I was not prepared to handle that."

I was still puzzled. "Has someone been too pushy? Have you been offended?"

"No, no, to the contrary. People are so kind here, so genuinely caring. I'd never experienced such love and concern before. In spite of myself, I've been gradually drawn into the spiritual atmosphere.

"You see," she continued, "my healthy, fit, fun-loving husband was killed in a senseless accident just a few weeks before he planned to retire. I was angry, and I blamed God. What kind of God would take such a good man and leave a faithful, loving wife all alone? I was angry, resentful, and bitter. No more God for me! No more prayers, church, or religion. I was finished—forever!

"I settled into a very self-indulgent lifestyle. I got up when I pleased, ate whatever and whenever I wanted, and went wherever I felt like going. I hated the world and withdrew from family and friends. I just wanted to be left alone.

"Those years were not good years. I gained 64 pounds; my blood pressure went up; I developed gout and began having angina. As I nursed my bitterness and anger, I continued going down. I guess I was more or less waiting to die." Wanda stopped talking and smiled, her eyes shining and her face full of joy.

"Something pretty dramatic must have happened. Is that what you want to tell me?"

"Yes. I began to really like it here. I gradually let myself relax and feel again, weep, sing, laugh, and even open the door of my mind a tiny crack to thoughts about Jesus Christ. Then my best friend in the class committed her life to Christ. I observed her joy, strength, and peace. I knew my own healing would not be complete unless I uprooted the bitterness and anger in my own heart.

> **People here believe in God, have faith, pray, sing, and love you earnestly, no matter how obnoxious you are! I was not prepared to handle that.**

"So I began to analyze my attitude toward God. I now saw it as a silly, futile effort to get even, to punish God for not being the heavenly Santa Claus I expected. I began to realize He is truly loving, fair, and just, and that I must learn to trust Him, even when I don't understand. I've decided to come back to the Lord."

We hugged and prayed and rejoiced together over Wanda's decision. She finished the program with joy. Many physical benefits came along too—weight loss, normalized blood pressure without medication, and disappearance of angina.

"I feel better than I have in years—physically, mentally, emotionally, and spiritually," she told me the day she left. "I'm glad I didn't know what the place was like, because I'm now busy thanking God I came."

SIX MONTHS LATER

During a period of stress Wanda developed severe chest pain and landed in a hospital intensive-care unit, where the angiogram she'd tried to avoid was done. She dreaded the verdict, but her cardiologist approached her with a big smile.

"No heart attack," he said. "What's more, the arteries that were clogging three years ago are clearing up now. Whatever it is you're doing, keep on doing it. I don't think you'll need heart surgery after all."

Suddenly on cloud nine, Wanda realized all the "sacrifices" she'd made to stay on a strict NEWSTART program were paying off.

See "Failure Is No Big Deal" (Section 8, Story 1).

The NEWSTART Restarters:

The Second Touch

When I come back and see others who have failed as badly as I have, it gives me courage to try again.
—A NEWSTART Restarter.

One blind man did not see perfectly after Jesus first touched him. But his sight was fully restored after the Master's second touch. Many NEWSTART alumni also need a "second touch" experience. These brave people turn up from time to time because they have gone through a period of regression, or because they feel they have failed completely. But they have the guts to come back and face everyone, soak up renewed inspiration, and determine to get back on the NEWSTART wagon once more.

As one man put it: "After I got better, it was hard to remember how sick I really had been. I began to slip here and there, and became weaker."

The common thread running through nearly every instance of discouragement and regression is a *crisis*. It can be physical, circumstantial, emotional, financial, spiritual, or a combination of these. The person becomes overwhelmed with too many battles to fight at once. And after the crisis passes, he or she is drained, weary, and often feeling discouraged and defeated. Many become sick.

The solution? NEWSTART principles are the best weapons to use. During a crisis the body needs more care than usual. Eating a simple diet and exercising actively will go far in combating the harmful effects of a crisis. Reaching out to a powerful, loving God will help ensure that you emerge from your crisis a stronger, better person.

Here are the stories of some of our courageous restarters.

Feeling Fit

STORY 1:

Failure Is No Big Deal

Beverly was coping. Unlike fat, humiliation doesn't show. She chatted easily and laughed often as she made her way through the registration procedures. Underneath her courageous smiling exterior, however, her heart was breaking. She had been a failure. Not just an ordinary failure, but a spectacular one. Failure was not a familiar feeling in her life. Coming back to this place was about the hardest thing she'd ever done.

Beverly had been a happy, energetic woman who breezed through life in high gear. "After all," she told Bud, her husband, "I've outlived Mama and Grandma by a good 10 years. They both died early of heart disease, but I feel just fine."

But Beverly wasn't "just fine." One day, flat on her back from an injury, she finally faced reality—high blood pressure, overweight, a dangerously high cholesterol. It was time for action. With determined dedication she enrolled in the NEW-START program. She must get well! And 25 days later she felt like a new woman. Hers was the big success story. Her radiant face and her fit, healthy body were impressive testimonials. For two years she was Exhibit A for anyone interested in healthful lifestyle changes.

But then came the fall. A family crisis took her away from home for an extended period. Stress, anxiety, and weariness took their toll. Her routines were disrupted and her new habits neglected. An inner voice called her from time to time, and promises were made, broken, remade, and broken again. As her goals receded, so did her motivation. Weeks melted into months, then years.

On the golf course one afternoon Beverly took a hard swing at a small ball that seemed to symbolize her mounting frustrations. A sudden blinding pain landed her back in bed. It was like a flashback to four years earlier. The weight was back, the blood pressure up. And golf, her cherished hobby, was now a literal pain. How could she have let this happen? The realization was a bitter pill. So this was Exhibit A! She'd let everyone down. The pain of humiliation overshadowed her physical suffering. Mrs. Perfect wasn't perfect at all. She would have to admit it—to herself and to others.

The Second Touch

Beverly came back to NEWSTART Lifestyle Center. She resumed the routine, the walks, the lectures, the food, the treatments. And again she got better. During our consultation I encouraged her to be less perfectionistic and more realistic. "You must stop being so obsessed with doing everything 100 percent," I told her. "When you do that, you set yourself up for failure. No one can measure up to such high standards all the time." Her new humility and her willingness to try again made her more receptive to our teaching. "After all," I reminded her, "a 10 percent improvement is better than no improvement."

> **I'm a wiser woman now. I'm not out for the big win. It's going to be one day at a time. God instructs His followers to forgive each other.**

The day came for our last office visit. "I'm a wiser woman now," she told me. "I'm not out for the big win. It's going to be one day at a time." She looked out the window, reflecting on her situation, then turned to me again. "Failure is no big deal, you know. One big binge will no longer defeat me." Her blue eyes softened. "My secret is that I'm enlisting outside help. I can relate to a God who instructs His followers to forgive each other at least 490 times. I still have a ways to go!"

We hugged and prayed together. It was our last visit, and we would soon part. I walked back to the lodge with her. "Four years ago I went home with only seven of the natural remedies," she mused. "This time I'm taking the eighth one home too: trust in divine power. That's the one that will make all the difference."

STORY 2:

I Became Totally Irrational
by Joan Hardy (name supplied)

I was what the doctors call "morbidly obese." What horrible words! I felt OK. But my husband pressured me into coming to NEWSTART. After I started the program, I fell in love with the place. I was impressed with the lifestyle and began to take some positive steps. (My husband came with me. I really thought he needed the program worse than I did. But he's stubborn—he wouldn't admit it.) I really worked with the program for about six months. I lost 40 pounds and began to feel a lot better.

Then I hit a snag and "fell off the wagon." Once off, it's extremely hard to get back on. By this time my husband had become a firm believer and was benefiting greatly. I would cook him all the good food every day, and then I'd fill up on junk. It's hard to explain; it's embarrassing; it's totally irrational! But it's what happens to many of us, especially those of us who have a very long way to go.

Since I am fairly young, I seemed to be fine for quite a while. But the body can take only so much abuse. My joints began to hurt. It was harder to walk, harder to do my work. My blood pressure crept up. A painful, gouty arthritis flared up. Diabetes showed its ugly head, then a painful stomach ulcer. I was living on medication! It wasn't worth it. It was too big a price to pay. This time my husband didn't have to push me. I'm the aggressor this time, and I mean business. I want to live. I want my health. God wants me to have these things. I'm determined to take God with me into this restart. The really sad part is that all this suffering would have been totally unnecessary if I had just stuck to the program I started three years ago! What a price to pay for stubborn pride.

STORY 3:

I Still Hate the Diet . . .
by Francis Miller

I knew I wouldn't live a year. I dreaded getting up in the morning. My life revolved around my medications—all 19 pills that I faithfully swallowed each day to survive. Survive for what? I often wondered. I couldn't do anything. I was weak and tired all the time and had no more interest in life. I watched my wife mow the lawn, watched life swirling around me.

Four years before, at age 60, I had bypass surgery. I went back to my job in the police department. I had a lot of hope—for a year. Then I started going downhill and had to quit my job. I became weaker and weaker. I put on a lot of weight and grew depressed. A friend told me about the NEWSTART program, and out of desperation I went. It was my last hope.

But for me, NEWSTART became the core of a new life. Within a year I had lost 80 pounds and increased my walking tolerance from less than a block to several miles. My blood pressure settled at 140/80, and I was off nearly all my medications.

My improvement continued. Soon I took the lawn mower away from my wife and cut the grass myself. I did roofing and other construction jobs. I went back to carpet laying. I worked all day, every day, enjoyed life, and felt great.

About four years after my NEWSTART experience, however, I had a series of upsetting problems that I allowed to interfere with my health habits. Quite a bit of weight crept back. I returned to the institution for inspiration and a restart.

> **I realize that I must live my new lifestyle carefully and conscientiously. The quantity and quality of my life depends on it.**

To be honest, I still hate the food. But what a small price to pay for my new life! Speaking of price, by saving the money I used to spend on medications, I've saved enough in less than three years to cover my entire expenses at NEWSTART.

I realize that I must live my new lifestyle carefully and conscientiously if my good results are to continue. My future, as well as the quantity *and* quality of my life, depends on it.

Author's Note: I was privileged to be present during NEWSTART's fourth annual homecoming when Francis Miller was chosen as the first president of the NEWSTART Alumni Association. Seeing him stand there, trim, tan, and radiant, I felt a profound sense of thanksgiving for what God is able to do for the precious people who come here and open up their lives to His way of life for them.

Francis Miller lived eight busy, happy, productive years following his NEWSTART experience.

STORY 4:

The Struggle Goes On
by Barbara Silva

My husband urged me to join a NEWSTART live-in program because he worried about my weight. To be honest, I was dangerously obese. Both of us ended up going through the program, with great benefit. My husband was more faithful than I was, but we both lost a lot of weight and felt really good.

Several years have passed since our NEWSTART experience. As time went on, stress and peer pressure weakened our resolve, and the pounds crept back. John went through two devastating surgeries with prolonged rehabilitation. Then he began developing symptoms of Alzheimer's disease. With all these things going on, I lost all control of my weight. By 1991 I tipped the scales at more than 300 pounds and felt lousy. But the Holy Spirit never gives up. I looked up my NEWSTART notes and recipes and restarted myself on the program. I've lost 88 pounds and have at least 88 more to go. My blood pressure is back to normal, and my diabetes is under control.

John is now in a nursing home, where I visit him every day. We sing, visit, and renew our love for Jesus and our longing for His soon return. Living alone is a difficult adjustment, but with God's help and the prayers of my brothers and sisters in Christ I will make it.

I wish I had a better report for John and me. But this is real life, and for most of us the struggle goes on. We learn to live one day at a time. Pray for us.

STORY 5:

Better Than Hawaii
by Stephanie Studnicki

I picked up the phone. "Stephanie, let's go to Hawaii for our vacation this year." It was one of my best friends calling.

Wonderful! I thought. *Just what I need.* I love living in Alaska, but because we are so far from everything, vacations are special. I'd had an intensely stressful year. I could use time in the sun and sand with warm breezes caressing my tired body.

But I didn't go to Hawaii. Instead I chose a 25-day restart at Weimar Institute. And for the third time, too! Why? Well, it isn't that I don't love Hawaii and the many other beauty spots in the world one can enjoy. When I go to these places, the same things always happen: I eat too much, lie around too much, think about myself, and indulge myself. I come away somewhat rested, but not feeling that much better.

My first NEWSTART experience was in 1978. I was really burned out. But after 25 days of simple food, exercise, early-to-bed and early-to-rise disciplined living—all the things we usually don't do on vacation—well, I just felt wonderful! I had a host of new, caring friends, and I renewed my relationship with a God who loves me very much. I cannot measure the blessings I received, both spiritual and physical. I can honestly say that no vacation I have ever taken has made me feel better than time spent at NEWSTART. I guess that's why I keep coming back!

Those of you who think you can't afford the price or can't take the time need to rethink your priorities. Instead of Aspen or Mammoth or the Bahamas, invest in a NEWSTART experience. It will be the best thing you've ever done for yourself. I'll guarantee that, and I'm not even a Seventh-day Adventist!

STORY 6:

No Bypass for Pete
by Pete Porfido

I had my first heart attack at age 51. A few months later I had a second one. I developed angina and borderline diabetes. I was also 50 pounds overweight. After appropriate testing, the doctors told me I was not a candidate for bypass surgery. Did that mean I was doomed? Right in the prime of my life? About that time I heard about Nathan Pritikin's program and went there. I improved and felt encouraged.

Several years later I found out about the NEWSTART program. I needed a restart, and since it was nearer my home, I joined the August 1980 NEWSTART class.

In the four years since, I have followed the program 85 to 90 percent. My weight came down to 147, a decrease of 53 pounds. I feel good, stay active, and enjoy life. I play golf, swim, and often take my boat out. I walk four to six miles a day. Also, I've quit alcohol.

There are a few things I can't do yet, such as play tennis and racquetball. And I've let my weight creep up a bit the last few months. That is why I especially wanted to come back to Alumni Homecoming Week. I'm soaking up inspiration for another restart. You'll see some changes for the better next year!

Author's Note: I heard from Pete in 1996, 15 years after his NEWSTART experience. He is now 72 years old. "I'm still 90 percent faithful to the program," he wrote. "I know that I owe my life to the NEWSTART principles. I'm taking no chances. I want to live!"

STORY 7:

Forty-five Cups of Coffee
by Verna Frosse

I was overweight, diabetic, hypertensive, depressed, and suicidal. I was drinking 45 cups of coffee a day to stay awake and keep going. And I was only 48 years old. My doctors couldn't seem to help. Regardless of what I did, I got no better. I prayed for a way out.

The answer came through a friend who told me about Weimar Institute. As I drove onto the campus I noticed the sign: NEWSTART lodge. I stopped and wept. That was what I longed for: a new start. The results after 25 days were nearly miraculous. I felt so good I wanted to shout from the rooftops, "Verna wants to live! God isn't finished with me yet!"

I went home highly motivated and did well for a time. But I must admit the day-by-day battle over the long haul isn't easy. Lifetime habits are nearly impossible to change. I know what I should do, but I need encouragement and support. I need a "shot in the arm" once in a while. That's why I'm here for a restart. Being with others, comparing notes, listening to lectures, walking the trails—all renew my inspiration.

Walking is not easy during the winter back home in Kansas. The windchill factor often goes well below zero. I pray daily that

The Second Touch

the Lord will give me the desire to walk. So far I've been faithful. Food is another big problem. I still have to fight a terrible compulsion to snack from the time I enter the house at 4:00 p.m. until I go to bed. It's been a lifelong habit, and it keeps defeating me. I need to surrender this problem to the Lord. That's the only way. Willpower alone is not enough. Please pray for me.

For the rest of Beverly's story, see Section 7, Story 1.

"SMOKING OR NON-SMOKING?"

The Deadliest Drug:
Your Choice

Do you have big ears? or curly hair? Is your nose too long, wide, pointed, or flat? Are you too short? There are many things in life about which we don't have a choice. So we live with them. There are other things, however, about which we do have a choice—such as whether or not to smoke. And we don't have to live with that.

Did you know that tobacco is the deadliest drug in the world? Every year it kills half a million Americans, more than all who die from AIDS, street drugs, fires, car crashes, and homicides combined.

Did you know that more smokers die from a heart attack than die from lung cancer?

And did you know that:

• smokers have much more cancer of the mouth, larynx (voice box), esophagus, pancreas, bladder, kidneys, and cervix than do nonsmokers?

• emphysema produces death by slow suffocation in 60,000 Americans a year as a result of smoking?

• statistically, each cigarette cuts 12 minutes off the normal life expectancy?

• more than 80 percent of lung cancers and 50 percent of bladder cancers could be prevented if people stopped smoking?

Smoking is the single most preventable cause of death in America.—U.S. Surgeon General.

Feeling Fit

STORY 1:
Violet's Last Chance

Small, wiry Violet Davis, usually a tornado of energy, was listless and depressed. She looked even smaller huddled in the big easy chair in her living room. It was time to come to terms with reality.

Reality for Violet meant that she wasn't going to live much longer unless some kind of miracle occurred. For the second time that day her phone had rung. And for the second time the few steps across her living room to pick it up had thrown her into a fit of coughing that left her so out of breath she could hardly talk. The same thing happened when she tried to walk to the bathroom. She coughed until she nearly passed out. Panic and fear edged into her consciousness and began to consume her. Dialing her sister, she told her that if the phone rang and all she could hear was someone gasping for breath, she should send the paramedics immediately.

Violet thought about her past. She had started smoking at age 15 and, with a few brief interruptions, had continued to smoke heavily for the next 50 years. Deep down she knew it wasn't good for her. She tried to quit several times. She went through the Schick program and attended a couple Five-Day Plans. One time she even had a friend drive her to a remote mountain cabin and leave her there for a week without her cigarettes. On the second day she hiked out to a service station for a fresh supply. Discouraged and feeling hopeless, she abandoned further attempts to quit.

Just before Christmas Violet caught a cold that promptly turned into pneumonia. She became so sick and short of breath that her doctor decided to hospitalize her. After spending Christmas in intensive care and remaining in the hospital well into January, she wasn't much better. Even the smallest exertion would bring on paroxysms of coughing that left her weak and struggling to breathe. Violet had grown up as a Christian, but over the years had neglected this area of her life. Now she raised her heart in prayer, pleading for direction.

That night she saw a short segment on the local TV news about a place called Weimar, a health institute of some sort. She wondered if she could find help there. After calling her doctor and receiving encouragement to go, she called the health center, only to find out she was too late for the January class. But she was accepted into the February class. Fearing she wouldn't live that long, Violet put her affairs in order and updated her will.

The night before she left for the health center, she threw all her cigarettes into the fireplace. As she drove to the institute the next morning, she firmly determined to stick with the program. It was her last chance. She knew if she blew it again, the curtains would come down on her life.

Violet felt better the moment she arrived. The fresh mountain air, the sunshine, and the friendliness of the people lifted her spirits. About 11:00 the next morning she was ushered into the treadmill room. Eyeing the contraption warily, she knew her test would be a dismal failure. She'd last a few seconds, maybe, at the most. But to her surprise, she was able to walk through three stages! Had a miracle happened already?

> **Violet had started smoking at age 15 and, with a few brief interruptions, had continued to smoke heavily for the next 50 years.**

It was explained to Violet that cigarette smoke contains nicotine, a narcotic that constricts small arteries, depriving the heart, lungs, brain, and other important areas of vital oxygen. Because she had not smoked for 36 hours, the nicotine in her body had been metabolized, and her small arteries were now able to carry more blood. Also, cigarette smoke contains carbon monoxide, a poisonous gas that blocks red blood cells and prevents them from picking up oxygen and carrying it to body cells. By now most of her red blood cells had been able to dispose of the carbon monoxide and resume carrying precious, needed oxygen. The improvement was so dramatic that Violet promptly began her walking program, and within a week she was able to average three to five miles a day on the trails.

The first few days were the hardest. She was given relaxing water treatments at night to help her sleep, and Turkish baths and other heat treatments during the day to help rid her body of the accumulated poisons. She discovered that the best way to stop a sudden craving for a cigarette was to go outside and walk. A drink of water and deep breathing also banished the urge. Another thing that proved helpful was the simple, almost bland food. The lack of spices and saltiness helped diminish the cravings.

By the end of the third week Violet felt better and more energetic than she had for years. She was laughing and joking and sleeping like a baby each night. At home she never thought of going to bed until after the 11:00 p.m. news. Here she couldn't seem to stay up past 8:30 p.m.!

Her family couldn't believe the change in her. Her sister and her niece quit smoking the week Violet returned home. She is once again her old self, a small tornado of energy. Although retired for several years, she wants to go back to her job. A pharmacist, she had operated her own drugstore for years. "It's a job I love," she told me. "But before I get tied down, I'm going to do some traveling. Last year I went to New Orleans, but coughed so badly I couldn't leave the hotel room. I finally tried one tour and sat coughing in the tour bus the whole time. Things are different now. I want to do something positive and useful. I thank God that my life has been given back to me."

STORY 2:

Peeking Into the Microscope
by C. S. Small, M.D., Pathologist

In normal human air passages the Creator installed a lining of cells that make a sticky material called mucus. Like old-fashioned flypaper, this mucus traps inhaled dusts and tobacco tar. The mucus, however, rides like a thin blanket on a thicket of tiny hairs called *cilia,* "eyelashes" that line the air tubes, or *bronchi.* The cilia move in concert, like the "wave" in the grandstand at the ballpark. What is more, they move backward slowly and forward faster so that the blanket of mucus, with trapped dust, tar, and other particles, gradually moves upward. Eventually it carries the trapped material far enough upward so that it can be spat out. So far, so good.

When a blast of tobacco smoke hits the surface of an air tube (bronchus), what happens to the cilia? They slow down and stop. And then what happens to the blanket of mucus with its burden of tar and dust? It stops ascending, and the tar begins to work on the cells lining the bronchus, eventually causing some of them to become cancer cells. With the cilia no longer able to cleanse the bronchial tubes, the smoker begins to cough.

The cancer transformation is not quick; it may take many years. But once a cancer begins, it steadily eats its way deeper into the lung, until by the time it is discovered, it is usually beyond surgical cure. To frustrate the beautifully designed cilia by smoking, allowing cancer to develop, is a disaster. As a "poet" has said:

The moral is, what God hath wrought;
To monkey with, we hadn't ought.

STORY 3:

The Genes Win One
by Gordon W. Thompson, M.D.

I straightened my tie and nervously adjusted the stethoscope around my neck. Was this *me,* the experienced, confidently competent, 36-year-old physician? Come *on!* The "terror" I faced on the other side of the door was only a tiny old woman. Maybe so, but I was still uneasy. The woman was 96 years old, and it was her first visit to a doctor of any kind. Her daughter, feeling it was time someone looked her over, had tricked her into my office.

Her mother had grown up on a tobacco farm, where folks worked from dawn till dusk. There she rolled her own cigarettes and often chewed tobacco leaves to relieve hunger. She'd outlived six husbands and borne six children at home without help of any kind. And this day she had walked into my office unassisted and with no complaints at all.

I took a deep breath and entered the examining room. My patient lay rather gingerly on the table, wrapped in the sheet like a mummy, eyeing me warily. Wondering how to start, I decided that checking her reflexes would be the least threatening thing I could do. I took out my little hammer and ran the tip of the handle across the bottom of her foot. She shot up like a volcano. "Sonny, don't you *ever* do that again!" The fire in her eyes and the reproach in her voice made me feel suddenly small and vulnerable. Somehow I finished the examination and escaped into my office. There really wasn't anything wrong with her. She was one of those rare persons born with a set of genes that rendered her practically indestructible.

"When do you want to see her again?" her daughter inquired anxiously.

I leaned back in my big chair. "I'd say in another 96 years would be about right."

STORY 4:

I Was Starving
by Lois Rohan

The day my weight reached 78 pounds, I changed my mind. I didn't want to die—I wanted to live! But was it too late? Was my body irreparably damaged? I wasn't starving myself to death for the usual reasons. I'd been a heavy smoker for 35 years. I couldn't quit. Five years earlier I had developed emphysema. The more I smoked and coughed, the worse it got. I grew pale, thin, and weak. Finally the doctor told me bluntly I was near the end. I must start carrying an oxygen tank around with me, because my lungs were failing.

I couldn't accept death by suffocation, so I decided starving to death would be easier. I felt grimly triumphant as the scales went down, down, down. I expected to die when I reached 75 pounds. Painlessly. Quickly.

But the day I reached 78 pounds, I suddenly wanted to live! I was only 52. I had two lovely daughters, grandchildren, a good business, a beautiful home. No, I didn't want to die! I looked for a place that would keep me away from cigarettes for a month and ended up in one of Weimar's NEWSTART programs. It was a struggle, but with help and prayers my cigarette cravings stopped. Breathing became much easier. At first it took 30 minutes for me to walk one half mile. Now I can do it in 13 minutes.

I'm busy planning a different future. No more pressured business lunches and junk food snacks. I'm going to take time to care for my health, enjoy friends, and drink in the beauty of life—the good life.

STORY 5:

The Hockey Player's Gold Mine

In the middle of a hockey game my arm started to hurt," Tom Walker was saying. "My elbow pad felt tight, so I slid it down. Later, going up some stairs, I felt the tightness again, this time across my chest as well. I blamed it on my cigarettes. After all, I was only 35 years old, quite solidly muscular, and led a very active life. Heart disease happens to older guys, I reassured myself, the ones who sit in stuffy offices and get fat. Most weekends found me riding my bicycle or motorcycle, playing hockey, or working out. How could I have heart trouble?

"But my smoking was something else. I knew it was hurting me. I had tried to stop at least 20 times without success. I started smoking at age 18 because it seemed to be the stylish, mature thing to do. After only three weeks of smoking, I developed an intense craving for it that never left. I need nearly two packs a day to satisfy me.

"Now I knew I needed help, but I kept putting it off. I was involved in six major business enterprises and felt I couldn't leave. Last summer I took off for Alaska to work in my gold mine, something I had looked forward to all year. But I couldn't do much. I was tired all the time, and the pain was almost constant. I finally gave up and came here. If you can help me gain freedom from my cigarette habit, it will be worth the time and money."

Nurse Larry Green met Tom at the airport. Tom still had a pack of cigarettes in his pocket, and as they walked to the baggage area, he asked when he was supposed to stop the cigarettes. Larry gave him a long look, then said, "Right now might be a good time." Tom tossed the pack in the trash can.

Arriving at NEWSTART Lodge an hour later, Tom was tired and nervous from the long trip and shaky from the lack of a cigarette. Larry anticipated this and took him directly to hydrotherapy and put him in the Russian steam bath. After sweating things out for a while, Tom told Larry he felt relaxed and refreshed. He slept well all night.

A few days later, when the tests were finished, Tom was told he had coronary artery heart disease with a disabling amount of angina.

"I was shocked," Tom told me later. "But I was also relieved to know I wasn't a hypochondriac after all."

Tom adjusted to the food and later pronounced it OK. "I began to see that the simplicity of the food and the lack of spices and salt contributed toward decreasing my craving for cigarettes. So did walks in the fresh, brisk air. In fact, when I wanted a cigarette, I would go out for a walk, and the craving would gradually dissipate."

During his NEWSTART program Tom learned to slow down. He got back in touch with his spiritual nature. "I became a born-again Christian six years ago, and I wanted to give my life totally to God. I quit booze, but it bothered me that I couldn't quit cigarettes.

"I thought back on my life. I'd been healthy and active until age 27. Then I took on more and more of a businessman's lifestyle with its stress and poor dietary habits."

When Tom went home, he changed his lifestyle completely. Besides conquering the tobacco habit, he severed himself from four of his six businesses. His life became much less hectic and pressured.

> **I'd been healthy and active until age 27. Then I took on more and more of a businessman's lifestyle with its stress and poor dietary habits.**

"I can honestly say I feel as I did in my 20s—no, actually as I did in my teens, before I started smoking. I now wake up each morning with a clear mind and zest for a new day. But I have one problem. Now I'm hooked on peanut butter! Do you have a cure for that?" he grinned.

Tom's father and grandfather had died of heart disease in their early 40s. Excited by his new knowledge of how to avoid such an outcome, Tom returned several months later, bringing his sister and his aunt and uncle to the NEWSTART program. He looked tan, relaxed, fit, happy—quite a contrast to the serious, pale, tense, depressed man of six months before.

"You know," he reflected, "I discovered a much better gold mine here than the one I have in Alaska! Really!"

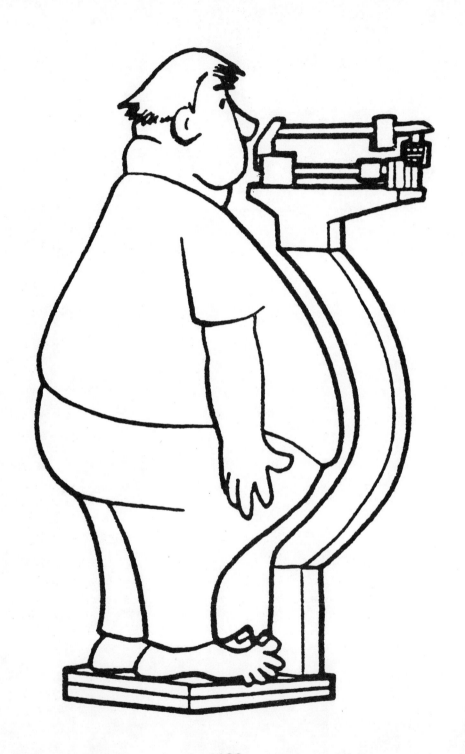

Health Professionals Evaluate NEWSTART:

The Ultimate Challenge

Faith? or presumption? Which is which? What's the difference? Where does one end and the other begin? Why didn't Jesus fling Himself from the pinnacle of the temple and demonstrate to the entire universe His total trust in God's power and protection? If a believer's faith can move mountains, why couldn't Jesus' faith carry him safely to the ground?

While every Christian faces continual variations of this temptation, physicians often meet it at its highest levels. When faced with life and death decisions, what to do? How far to go? When to stop? Which treatments or medications to use? Which to avoid?

Physicians meet the Jehovah's Witness who sincerely believes he or she will lose heaven for accepting a lifesaving blood transfusion. They meet the conscientious Seventh-day Adventist who refuses antimalarial drugs, only to be salvaged at great expense from a malignant form of the disease contracted while helping in a refugee camp. Physicians also meet people who abuse themselves or who exploit other people into buying expensive but unproven "natural remedies." And a few unscrupulous physicians exploit their own patients.

So what has this got to do with NEWSTART? NEWSTART programs present physicians with another important decision: whether or not to support such programs. Much as with pastors and church leaders, the credibility and reputation of physicians rest on their wise and cautious choices, their example, their being able to avoid extremes, and their ability to walk a balanced middle ground.

So we must understand why some very fine Seventh-day Adventist health professionals question NEWSTART results. I did too until I observed and experienced for myself what happens. And because the principles not only work, but are in har-

139

mony with the basics of the Adventist health message, my faith was such that I abandoned a lucrative practice and became a NEWSTART physician myself.

But laypeople need to realize that conventional medicine and lifestyle medicine are not in competition; they are meant to complement each other. It's not an either-or situation. As individuals we must look for the right kind of help. Just as God does not send angels to do surgery, give blood transfusions, or put a broken arm in a cast, neither does God magically change our moods, our habits, or our choices. We often need the help of professionals for these things.

I once sent the following lighthearted message to some physician friends in conventional medicine to help them understand how NEWSTART-type health professionals could lighten their load:

Breathes there a doc with time so free that he can help each patient see
Just how to lose his excess weight? And mend the fences with his mate?
And exercise his heart to par? And from his diet salt to bar?
And many, many other things—a helpless sense, that's what it brings!
—With apologies to Edward Everett Hale
"The Man Without a Country"

The 10 brief stories that follow will give you intimate glimpses into the thoughts and feelings of physicians and dentists who have come to "taste and see" for themselves what goes on in NEWSTART programs.

Sound too good to be true? I've honestly not heard a negative response yet!

The Ultimate Challenge

STORY 1:

I Was Very Skeptical
by Robert N. Brown, M.D.

When I arrived at Weimar Institute two years ago, I was very skeptical, to say the least. At first I challenged and argued over nearly everything they tried to teach me. But my hostilities quickly melted, and I became tremendously interested in what I was observing.

I'd had triple bypass surgery seven years before. I was doing fairly well, but wondered if I might not do even better on a conditioning program. I investigated Pritikin's Longevity Center, but was turned off by the price and their lack of hydrotherapy and physical therapy, not to mention the total absence of any spiritual atmosphere.

During my 25-day NEWSTART program my weight, cholesterol, and triglycerides all dropped nicely, but garden therapy nearly did me in. A half hour of shoveling manure reactivated an old tendonitis that hurt terribly for the next two weeks. The physical therapist worked on the painful areas, hurting me even more. But I'll have to admit that I've had no problems at all in the two years since.

I now feel that the critics of Weimar's health program are those who have not been there, have not tasted it for themselves, and are ignorant in what they say. I am 100 percent behind the program and would like to join the staff someday. I certainly recommend the NEWSTART program in my health lectures and to everyone I see who is interested and who needs it.

I'll admit that over the long term I've felt the diet to be too strict and often impractical. However, as a result of my compromises I'm fighting the weight battle again. My 93-year-old father-in-law, who went through the NEWSTART program with me, has followed it very conscientiously and is doing just great—better than I am. Last week he rode 10 miles on his bicycle.

Author's Note: Twenty-two years have elapsed since Dr. Brown's original bypass surgery and 16 years since his NEWSTART experience. Through the years he has enjoyed serving short terms as a volunteer missionary doctor overseas.

Now 82, Dr. Brown is presently battling a number of serious medical problems, including Parkinson's and cancer. "My weight is normal," he reported recently, "and I do eat healthfully. I'm still hanging in there and glad to be alive."

STORY 2:

The Medical Student

Working through translators was not new to me, but I'd never taught NEWSTART classes that way. My first experience was with Moses, a senior medical student from Korea. He was lots of fun and kept things lively, not only for the patients, but for the staff, as his inquiring mind challenged our knowledge.

"I've gotten a new perspective on medical treatment that I was not taught in medical school," he told us near the end of the session. "If I hadn't seen it happen for myself, I really would not have believed that blood sugars come down, elevated blood pressures normalize, cholesterol levels drop, and angina pains can disappear during NEWSTART programs. It's absolutely incredible that such basically simple lifestyle factors can initiate results like this in such a short time. It reminds me of the original Moses' encounter with the burning bush. Like him, I know I'll never be the same again either."

Author's Note: Dr. Moses Yun accompanied a group from Korea who came to the Mission Health Promotion Center in Muak Lek, Thailand, to participate in our 14-day NEWSTART program in 1994. Dr. Yun has since graduated from medical school and is now in residency training.

STORY 3:

Extreme Methods
by Ray Pellow, M.D.*

As a retired physician and conscientious Seventh-day Adventist, I had always been careful with my diet. I thought I knew all the answers. But when a heart attack laid me on the ground out in my orchard, I knew I had to make some drastic changes in my life.

My largely vegetarian diet was too rich, and my weight had crept upward. Also, I needed a consistent exercise program. But progress at home was slow and discouraging, and I became somewhat depressed. I realized I needed guidance and encouragement toward a much stricter lifestyle than I had previously thought necessary.

I knew about Weimar and enrolled in a NEWSTART program with considerable hope, but also with some apprehension and reservations. Right from the start I could see there were people in our group with serious health problems, including two diabetics, several hypertensives, and others with various heart problems. One had had previous bypass surgery, but was obstructing again. There were arthritics and people with claudication, drug dependency, and obesity. Nearly everyone suffered from serious levels of stress, and several were depressed.

As we finished our third week, I noticed that everybody— and I mean everybody—was getting better! When I arrived, between my angina and my arthritis I could hardly get around at all. Even a few steps were painful. Now I was walking several miles a day, losing weight, and feeling good.

And I was impressed with the high standards of medical practice. The doctors, nurses, and other medical personnel are highly trained, up-to-date, and solidly scientific. I now see that theirs is by far the most promising way of treating the degenerative diseases, especially diabetes, hypoglycemia, and vascular disease. Are the methods extreme? Yes, but they need to be. I've never had this kind of success in treating these diseases in private practice.

And another thing: When I came, hardly anyone except the staff paused to say grace before their meals. Before the month ended, I noticed everyone was doing it. That's the kind of subtle spiritual influence that surrounded us.

---

* Now deceased.

STORY 4:

Reality Was Better

by D. Clifford Ludington, M.D.

Having married a NEWSTART physician, I felt certain I knew everything it was possible to know about Weimar Institute's health program. But after experiencing a 10-day live-in program for health professionals and pastors, I want to say that it is even better in reality. I feel this program should be a requirement, not only for physicians and pastors, but for church administrative personnel as well, especially those who must spend long, sedentary hours indoors. It is God's will that we be healthy, physically as well as spiritually.

I can attest from my own experience that when we understand and implement God's revealed health principles, He can bless us with improved efficiency and well-being. In the 18 months that I have implemented these principles in my own life, I have lost 45 pounds. My health has improved so much I recently qualified for a *decrease* in insurance premiums.

In this life disappointment is the crop we most often reap when we harvest our expectations. However, I feel safe in guaranteeing that following God's plan for living via the eight health laws embodied in programs such as NEWSTART will surely exceed your expectations, too. You'll say, as I do, "The reality is better."

Author's Note: Since writing this story 15 years ago, Dr. Ludington, an orthopedic surgeon, has remained vigorous and healthy. He retired in 1992 at age 70 and has devoted his time since then to spreading the good news of good health in several countries. At the time of this writing, he is serving a two-year term as a NEWSTART volunteer physician for the Mission Health Promotion Center in northeastern Thailand.

In this life disappointment is the crop we most often reap when we harvest our expectations. Following God's plan will exceed your expectations.

The Ultimate Challenge

STORY 5:

I Was Critical
by Robert Sperazza, M.D.

I was a third-year medical student at Loma Linda University when I joined a 10-day NEWSTART program at Weimar Institute. I wasn't sure what I would find when I got there. I wasn't sick, so I wasn't expecting to get well.

I came to learn, but like most students, I was critical. I was particularly attuned to the smallest hint of fanaticism or to the misuse of scientific data. However, after 10 days I could honestly say I liked the basic concept. The diet and lifestyle that NEWSTART stands for are good medicine. The concepts may seem radical, but they work.

This was the first time I had seen a sincere and successful effort to apply sound medicine and biblical principles to society's medical needs, while carefully avoiding fanaticism.

STORY 6:

A Dentist Reflects on NEWSTART
by William D. Cuff, D.D.S.

Like so many of us who grew up Adventist, I thought I was doing everything right in regard to my health. I didn't smoke or drink; I avoided caffeine, rarely ate meat, and watched my sugar intake carefully.

Still, as time went on I ate richer foods and exercised less, and my weight crept up. In 1976 I landed on the operating table for bypass heart surgery. Fortunately, I had a cardiologist who realized the bypass wasn't the total answer. He was anxious that I modify my lifestyle so that not only would the arterial damage stop and my bypass last, but also I could avoid future vascular complications.

I came to Weimar's NEWSTART program in its early days. In fact, I was a member of the third class. I brought my wife with me, as she was not well at the time. From the moment we arrived, we both loved the place, the program, and the people.

We went home feeling younger and better than we had in years. Our church members and family noticed the difference immediately and wanted to know all about what had happened.

It has been nearly four years since my NEWSTART experience. My health has remained good, and I'm working full-time. My compliance with the program hasn't been perfect, and my weight is creeping up again, but my life and health have certainly been much better because of what I learned and the changes I've made.

One of the hardest things for us in carrying out the principles consistently at home has been the "convenience foods." In these pressured times it's so easy to reach for prepared and processed foods to save time. Eating out is another problem. There is very little one can find, even in the best restaurants, that isn't detrimental to health. Also, we need "refresher times." It gets harder to maintain a high degree of motivation as time goes on.

But I'm convinced of several things. I've noticed that the young people who exercise regularly and take an interest in their health are the ones who are the most active in the church and the most interested in spiritual things. This applies to us older ones too! Kathy and I know from experience how much better we feel and how much happier and more efficient we are when we stick closely to the health principles we know.

I'm 100 percent behind everything NEWSTART stands for. I'm glad for these few days of "refreshing." It has given me the renewed inspiration and motivation I need to get back to work on those extra pounds!

Author's Note: It has been 18 years since Bill's NEWSTART experience. He assures me he still can't say enough good things about what the NEWSTART principles have meant to the quality of both his physical life and his spiritual life. At age 72 he feels fine and continues his busy dental practice.

The Ultimate Challenge

STORY 7:

I Needed Motivation
by Charles L. Yeager, M.D.

I have been practicing neurology and psychiatry for 34 years and just recently retired. I was having a few cardiac symptoms and had picked up some extra weight. I read Mr. Pritikin's book and became very interested in what he was doing. Then I heard Weimar Institute had a similar program. I have always been reasonably careful of my health, but realized I could do a lot better. My wife and I needed motivation and some know-how in practical ways of improving our lifestyle.

The NEWSTART program is a carefully disciplined one, with activities prescribed according to individual needs and tolerances. Perhaps the best benefit for us was getting on a food program that is health-building. Was the food good? Well, there are several definitions of enjoyment. The absence of salt made many things seem rather tasteless at first. But we quickly became accustomed to it, and soon found the food tasty and enjoyable.

On this program we felt better quickly—the entire body and mind improved rapidly. Our walking tolerance increased daily, and we felt less and less stressed and tired. My blood pressure, which registered 180/96 the day I arrived, quickly settled down to 110/60. I also lost seven pounds. Another thing I appreciated was being told exactly what my test results were, what they meant, and what to do about them.

The spiritual emphasis was most important. For most of us there is too little emphasis on our spiritual needs in times of sickness and trouble. I strongly agree with all the things that are being taught and done in the NEWSTART program.

STORY 8:

I Came to Observe
by Vincent Gardner, M.D.

I came to the NEWSTART program as a professional observer, because I was looking for better ways to teach and put into effect the health principles advocated by Adventists. I was impressed with the practical way these principles are handled. First we sit in class and learn the physiological basis. Then we apply what we learn—in the cafeteria, on the trails, in every aspect of our lives. I appreciate the tender, loving attention each patient receives and like the way the doctors and nurses are always available, night and day. There is an EKG ready to go the minute it is needed, as well as a defibrillator and other emergency equipment.

Results here are much better than can be achieved in private practice. For 26 years I tried to teach my patients how to eat, exercise, and live. I invested weeks in my effort to motivate them, with marginal success. I can see the advantages of getting people away from their home environment and their problems and allowing them to experience for themselves what healthful lifestyle changes can accomplish in even a few days.

I am 100 percent in harmony with all that is done here. For most people, making lasting lifestyle changes seems to be as impossible as a leopard changing its spots. But the good news is that with God's help people *can* change, both physically and spiritually.

———

Author's Note: Dr. Gardner sent this update in a February 28, 1996, letter. He wrote, It's been 15 years since I came to Weimar Institute as a professional observer. Marilyn and I returned to New York and worked with the van center for the next eight years. When it came time to retire, I was invited to be chaplain for the NEWSTART program at Weimar, a position I held for two years. And then, four years ago, I became coordinator for the professional observer program, a position I still hold.

I am making a special effort to attract medical students, residents, and practicing physicians to a NEWSTART-type program. They need an understanding of lifestyle medicine if they are going to treat today's killer diseases successfully .

I am more convinced than ever of the effectiveness of this program.

The Ultimate Challenge

STORY 9:

The Root of Health
by Sang Lee, M.D.

I consider trust in divine power to be the most important factor necessary for true healing. A for-real relationship with the true God, our Creator, is never optional to health—it is the very root of health. Trust in God has profound effects on both the physical mechanisms of the body and the workings of the mind.

For example, I believe that joyful trust in God enables Him to increase and harmonize beneficial neurohormones, such as the endorphins and possibly serotonin. Research studies indicate that the rise of such levels benefits one's total health. These hormones have a great calming, relaxing influence, bringing deeper restorative sleep, reducing depression, strengthening the immune system, controlling pain, and stabilizing one's emotions. All of these factors are crucial to healing of any kind.

Without trust in God, the mind is often plagued with fears, doubts, and anger. These stress factors are associated with rising adrenaline and corticoid levels that relate to tension, a rise in blood pressure, increased fatigue, and insomnia, and they can even hinder the effectiveness of medications. Living without trusting in God is like walking on a dark night with no lights—every step is a harrowing experience.

Trust in divine power means getting to know God well enough to trust Him for present and future well-being.

Many people can—and do—find successful healing on a purely physical level. But without a trusting relationship with the God from whom the healing truly comes, all the other measures, including NEWSTART remedies, give only a temporary solution to the body's needs. But when trust is added, God can do so much more. He can multiply the benefits received from other remedies, and He can extend healing into all dimensions—the physical, mental, emotional, and spiritual. This is why I say that genuine health comes from one's relationship with the true God.

Feeling Fit

What does trust in divine power mean? Simply that people open their minds and hearts to God's love and mercy and allow His healing power to flow into their lives. It means getting to know God well enough to trust Him for present and future well-being. The Bible says that "A merry heart doeth good like a medicine: but a broken spirit drieth the bones" (Prov. 17:22). Health isn't just eating and drinking and exercising. It is also "righteousness, and peace, and joy in the Holy Ghost" (Rom. 14:17).

NEWSTART and Diabetes:

Not a Losing Battle

Diabetes has been a confusing and frustrating disease, difficult to understand even among medical professionals. Because the body is unable to handle glucose (sugar) that builds up to dangerous levels in the blood, most of the focus in this century has been directed toward keeping carbohydrate (sugar and starch) intake low and producing more effective types of insulin.

More recent experiments have turned up a new and surprising finding: the relationship of diabetes to fat. For example, Dr. James Anderson, a respected world authority on diabetes, reported some interesting experiments. Dr. Anderson was able to turn lean, healthy, young men into mild diabetics in less than two weeks by feeding them a rich, 65 percent fat diet. A similar group, fed a lean 10 percent fat diet plus one pound of sugar per day, did not produce even one diabetic after 11 weeks, when the experiment was stopped.

There are two types of diabetes. Type I, insulin-dependent diabetes melitus (IDDM), commonly called juvenile diabetes, usually occurs in childhood or youth and is often hereditary. These diabetics cannot survive without insulin. About 5 to 10 percent of diabetics are Type I.

Type II, non-insulin dependent diabetes melitus (NIDDM), is called adult-onset diabetes, because it generally hits around midlife as people get older and fatter. Type II diabetics usually have plenty of insulin, but something blocks its action. About 90 to 95 percent of diabetics are Type II.

NEWSTART principles produce near-miraculous results with Type II diabetes. A high-fiber, very low-fat diet helps activate the body's natural insulin, and blood sugar levels fall, sometimes quite rapidly. Most adult-onset diabetics are overweight, and normalizing weight is often all it takes to reverse their disease.

Feeling Fit

In the stories that follow, you will notice that Sandy (p. 155) has Type I diabetes. On a strict NEWSTART program she needs less insulin, and her diabetes is easier to control. The rest of the stories concern adult-onset (Type II) diabetes and illustrate the ways in which the NEWSTART principles work together to help solve the problems.

STORY 1:

I Wanted to Go to Rio . . .
by Melvin Seard

I really wanted to go to Rio de Janeiro. The president of my company and a number of delegates were going there to meet leaders from other countries. As head of security, my job was to arrange for their safety and protection and to oversee the operation once we arrived. It was not only an exciting assignment, but also the chance of a lifetime to see one of the world's most beautiful cities.

However, I was having serious health problems. I was overweight, my blood pressure was too high, and even daily injections of 52 units of insulin were not controlling my diabetes. I'd had these problems for 17 years, but despite following everything the doctors told me to do, I kept getting worse. As the time neared for the trip, I felt so sick and discouraged I knew there was little chance I could go.

My friend Bob Spangler* had just returned from a health center out West and urged me to go there. I was only 49 years old and not ready to be tossed on the shelf just yet. So after praying about it, I determined to go and fight for my life.

At NEWSTART I faced a new diet, new concepts of health, and a new lifestyle. I'd been careful about sugar for years, but now I was taken off all refined and processed foods, as well as all animal products. I learned how important a high-fiber diet is for diabetics, because it helps stabilize blood sugar levels. I learned how critical weight control is in the management of diabetes. More than that, I learned how to get my weight down and keep it down. Excess fat plays a pivotal role in adult-onset diabetes, as it seems to paralyze the insulin, making it less effective. I found that my very low-fat, high-fiber diet allowed me

154

to eat a higher volume of food with fewer than half the calories I was used to. Even with my heavy exercise program of walking and hiking as much as 15 miles a day, I never felt hungry at all. Additionally, exercise helped me lower my blood pressure, lose weight, reduce my insulin needs, banish depression, condition my body, and give me a sense of well-being.

At the end of 25 days the results were so amazing that I wouldn't have believed them if they hadn't happened to me. I lost 22 pounds, my blood pressure was normal without medication, and—praise the Lord—my blood sugar was staying within normal limits without any insulin! After 17 years I was like a man out of prison—free at last. I couldn't remember ever feeling better in my life. And I did go to Rio—feeling great and functioning well!

It's been six months now, and I've lost a total of 35 pounds, bringing me to my normal weight. I walk faithfully seven miles a day—rain or shine. I joined a gym so that when the weather is bad I can work out there. My blood sugar and blood pressure remain normal, and I continue to feel like a young man. I wish I could tell the world about this lifestyle! Just feeling so good would be worth the whole program. But I have the added bonus of my diseases going into remission and . . . I went to Rio!

Author's Note: It's been more than 10 years since Melvin's NEWSTART experience. He assured me in a recent phone call that he is still on the job and doing quite well.

---

*See Section 3, Story 1.

STORY 2:

Diabetes at Age 17

Sandy (not her real name) was a typical American child, raised on a typical American diet of corn flakes, milk, white bread with jam, far too many sweets, and too few nutritious vegetables. She liked to read, sew, and play the piano, so her lifestyle was more sedentary than it should have been. She never worried about her health, although she had several relatives who were quite obese and had something called "diabetes." Sandy didn't even know what that word meant.

Feeling Fit

During her last two years in high school Sandy noticed that she could eat large amounts of food without gaining weight. "I just thought I was one of those fortunate people with a high metabolism," she says.

But by her seventeenth birthday Sandy had to face the fact that she had diabetes, the kind she'd have to live with for the rest of her life. "I know the Lord helped me, because I accepted the disease and saw it as a challenge. I followed the diet the ADA [American Diabetes Association] prescribed at that time and began a vigorous aerobic exercise program. I did well for a while."

By the time she finished college, Sandy's diabetes had edged out of control. Because of this, she was unable to go on to graduate school. "I was keenly disappointed and began to harbor self-pity and resentment toward this disease I couldn't seem to control. I became so depressed and bitter that I blamed God for giving me the disease. I nursed my misery for about a year. Then one day I had a dramatic confrontation with the Holy Spirit and could finally see how self-centered and unproductive my life had become. I went to God for help."

> **By her seventeenth birthday Sandy had to face the fact that she had diabetes, the kind she'd have to live with for the rest of her life.**

Through several providential happenings, Sandy came to work at Weimar Institute as a secretary. What she learned there, along with information she read in Ellen White's book *Counsels on Diet and Foods,* motivated her to stop using milk, eggs, oil, and cheese. Sandy was already a vegetarian, and she also eliminated most processed and refined foods. Her daily insulin requirement decreased from 55 to 32 units per day. Sandy continued to exercise in earnest—walking, jogging, and cross-country skiing.

"About a year later I made another change," Sandy told us. "I switched from the 'preventive' diet to the more strict 'reversal' diet.* I also began eating two meals a day instead of three. Within two months I lost 20 pounds and not only reduced my insulin dosage again, but I needed only one injection a day instead of two.

"Dealing with diabetes is not easy, especially when you are

young. But God has taken away the bitterness and frustration I once felt. He helps me live day by day without becoming overwhelmed by my problems. I can say now that I'm excited to see God working in my life, helping me grow physically, mentally, and spiritually as I learn to cooperate with Him and His health laws."

———

*For details on diets, see Appendix 2.

STORY 3:

A Bit of Heaven on Earth

We urgently need a physician for our NEWSTART program in Thailand," the letter read. "Will you come?"

"Let's go, Aileen," my husband responded, even though we had just moved into our retirement home.

Soon afterward a weary, sweating, jet-lagged couple of volunteer missionaries dragged into Mission Health Promotion Center (MHPC)*, looking for a cool place to get some sleep. Instead, we were greeted by 18 smiling, cheerful, energetic Koreans ready to begin their NEWSTART experience. *Koreans in Thailand?*

"Yes," bright-eyed little Mrs. Park explained. "The good reputation of this health center has spread to Korea. We all bought tickets and flew to Thailand, hoping to improve our health."

I learned some fascinating facts about Korea from Pastor Phillip Yun, who accompanied the group. While only three to four percent of the 3.4 billion people in Asia are Christians, in South Korea 25 percent of the population is Christian. Of these, approximately one of every 500 is a Seventh-day Adventist, about 125,000 altogether. What makes the difference? Often suffering helps open people's hearts to the gospel, and the Koreans certainly suffered under 35 years of brutal occupation by the Japanese (1910-1945).

Also accompanying Pastor Phillip were his medical student son, Moses, who served as translator, two cooks, and the tour director. Of the 13 patients, three were Adventists, eight were Christians of other denominations, and two, a retired university professor and his wife, were atheists. Mrs. Park was not only the eldest in the group, she was also the one with the most serious health problems.

Feeling Fit

"I've suffered from diabetes for 12 years," she told me. "At first I tried to control the disease by diet, but it kept getting worse. Four years ago I began injecting insulin, 35 units every day, but it hasn't helped much. My eyesight is deteriorating and my feet and legs are getting numb. Since I am a Christian woman, I began praying to God for help. When I heard about this place, I felt it might be an answer to my prayers."

Mrs. Park adjusted well to our program. The volunteer Korean cooks endeavored to produce low-fat, high-fiber vegan** meals to suit Korean tastes. Brown rice was accepted quite well, but the Koreans really missed their usual kimchi, a special kind of fermented cabbage, used daily to season their food. They were good sports about our blander version of this choice food, but complained that some Thai dishes were "too spicy."

Mrs. Park didn't complain about anything. She began walking in the morning and covered seven tenths of a mile the first day. On the tenth day she walked 4.2 miles and still felt good. She learned to test her own blood sugar and to adjust her insulin dosage accordingly.

Midway through the second week, Mrs. Park telephoned her daughter. "My blood sugar came down to nearly normal after four days," she reported. "Now I have stopped injections completely and need only a small daily dose of insulin by mouth. I can't believe how good I feel. It is so beautiful and peaceful here; it's like a bit of heaven on earth. I know God led me to this place, because I now understand my disease and know how to take care of myself. I plan to live this way the rest of my life."

The medical staff weren't the only people busy during the 14 days. Pastor Phillip conducted morning worships and evening programs for the group. He walked with the patients, shared meals, and spent personal time with them. On the final Sabbath four people took their stand for Jesus Christ and were baptized in our Jacuzzi, including the atheistic university professor.

"You Adventist people are so right about health principles," he said, "that I feel confident you are right about religion, too."

I asked his wife how she felt about her husband's baptism. She smiled at my naïveté. "I'm ready to be baptized too," she replied. "But it's the custom in Korea to let the husband go first."

Not a Losing Battle

What a start to our volunteer mission service! If we'd had any doubts before, we knew now that this was where God wanted us.

---

*MHPC is a NEWSTART residential facility, located 90 miles from Bankok in a beautiful resort setting.

**A term used to differentiate lacto-ovo vegetarians from those who use no animal products at all.

STORY 4:

Back From the Edge

I'm diabetic, and I'm out of control." Janet Zielke's eyes were heavy with worry. "This morning as I drew up my morning insulin, I fingered the syringe, thinking, *Why not take the whole bottle? Wouldn't it be a painless shortcut to oblivion?* The possibility seemed such a welcome thought . . . I felt frightened! What was happening to me? It scared me into coming for help.

"I've really been trying to watch my diet," she went on, "but I'm still needing several doses of insulin a day. And despite conscientious checking on my glucometer [a device that measures blood sugar from a drop of fresh blood], I keep having insulin reactions."

We were sitting in my tiny office in a corner of the newly opened Norwalk Adventist Health Center. Norwalk is a suburb of Los Angeles, and the local church, dedicated to an inner-city health ministry, had already started a bakery and health food store next door. Janet was one of our first patients. Her tired eyes and sluggish movements screamed depression, and her overweight, middle-aged body bulged in her nondescript cotton housedress. It would be a long day. I was not overjoyed.

But Janet wasn't just another obese, depressed, middle-aged woman. She was a whole encyclopdia of diseases, all of them serious. She was 40 pounds overweight and she was short of breath. Her blood pressure measured 240/120. Her blood chemistries indicated a considerable degree of kidney failure, not an uncommon finding in diabetics. Janet was also a highly intelligent, creative, affluent business woman. She had once been the buyer for a very respected department store. She and her husband owned a flourishing business.

As gently as I could, I explained the seriousness of her problems and what she needed to do. When tears formed in her eyes, I feared I'd said too much.

"This isn't news to me," she said sadly. "I really know better than to have let myself get into this condition. You see, two years ago I spent one month in a Napa Valley health center. I lost weight, my blood pressure came down, my blood sugar stabilized, and I was able to stop insulin. When I left, I felt great, like a new woman. I knew that was the right way to live, the lifestyle I needed.

"Problems started, however, almost as soon as I got home. I work full-time with my husband in our business, and we are in the habit of eating out or ordering in at least twice a day. It became harder for me to stick to the right food, and after a while I gave up trying. I neglected my exercise, and my weight crept back up.

"As my health went down, so did my spirits. I've never had much self-confidence anyway, and many things happen to women in midlife to knock their confidence even lower. My life became a burden, and I often wondered if it was really worth it to struggle on. But it was the episode with the syringe this morning that shocked me into facing reality. It's ironic that I really basically know what to do. But I need medical supervision. I need guidance and encouragement along the way. I need to be sure I'm doing everything correctly and safely."

> **I called Janet's doctor about her kidney failure. He knew about it but hadn't told her. He felt it was just a matter of time until she would need dialysis.**

Janet's first appointment lasted two hours. She was delighted to find that our program was very similar to the one that had produced such good results for her before.

Five days later Janet was all smiles. "My insulin reactions have stopped," she reported. "My blood sugar is leveling out already, and I've lowered my insulin dosage. But I'm curious as to why it's happening so fast. I've made only a few dietary changes so far."

"You've switched to a very low-fat, high-fiber diet," I reminded her. "When you eat unrefined plant foods, you get a good dose of insoluble fiber. In the body this kind of fiber takes on fluid and swells up like a sponge, which definitely helps you feel full and satisfied on fewer calories. And as the fiber makes its way through the intestines, its mass slows the absorption of nutrients into the blood stream, helping to level out the hikes and dips of your blood sugar. For the same reason, this kind of high-fiber diet also straightens out most hypoglycemics.

"Hunger is a very interesting concept. Most people believe hunger occurs when the stomach is empty. But what causes true hunger is a drop in a person's blood sugar level."

"So that's why I get so ravenous after an insulin injection!" Janet exclaimed. "Now that I need only an occasional dose, it's much easier to control my appetite."

Janet's high-fiber diet also helped her lose weight without feeling hungry. In six weeks she'd lost 20 pounds. She had what we call adult-onset diabetes (Type II), the kind that 90 percent of diabetics have. It usually begins around middle age, and its victims are almost all overweight. Type II diabetics differ from Type I diabetics, formerly called juvenile diabetics, in that Type I occurs in younger people and is often hereditary. These diabetics are usually thin. They make no insulin at all, and they will need insulin for life, or until surgeons are able to transplant the proper parts of a pancreas into their bodies successfully.

In adult onset (Type II) diabetics, insulin is usually present but is blocked. In recent years we've learned that normalizing the weight, eating a low-fat, high-fiber diet, and exercising regularly release blocked insulin. This is why many diabetics today are successfully reversing this disease by attention to lifestyle factors.

Once Janet got on the right diet, continued to lose weight, and exercised regularly, her diabetes became much easier to control. But she'd had the disease for a long time, and as a result, she had to cope with damaged kidneys, as well as damaged coronary arteries.

I called Janet's doctor about her kidney failure. He knew about it but hadn't told her. He felt it was just a matter of time until she would need dialysis. Kidney dialysis usually means that a person spends three to four hours a day, two or three times a week, having their blood circulated through a machine that does what the kidneys can no longer do. (Peritoneal dialysis is sometimes used in milder cases.)

I remembered our success at getting another patient out of kidney failure*, so we applied the same techniques to Janet. However, in her home setting, Janet responded so very slowly that we suggested a NEWSTART program at Weimar. When she and her husband realized the seriousness of the situation, they readily agreed and went there together.

Janet came home much improved and with considerably increased energy. She dressed well, and her step was lively. Her interest in life soared, and she involved herself in all sorts of interesting projects.

Janet had another surprise for me. "I am really a Seventh-day Adventist," she said one day. "I was brought up that way. Then the cares of the world crowded in on me and I got discouraged and dropped out." Then she brightened. "But things are different now. I'm back in church, giving my testimony about the lifesaving Adventist health principles every chance I get."

Janet's improvement lasted for two years. She kept assuring me that she was following her program carefully. Still, I noticed her blood pressure creeping up, and she was retaining fluid. I felt her intake of salt was considerably more than she admitted. One day she invited me to lunch at a restaurant. We both ordered soup, and she carefully instructed the waiter not to put salt in hers. Then I realized her problem. She was back to eating out and ordering in frequently. She relied on her tried-and-true suppliers not to salt anything! But what she didn't realize was that most restaurant food is prepackaged and presalted.

I talked to Janet about this problem. But her greatest earthly joy was being able to spend her days working at her adored husband's side or at a desk nearby. She just could not cope with preparing the kind of food she needed and still be her husband's companion in their business.

Just choose health? It sounds so easy, so desirable. But people have different priorities. To Janet, being with her husband outweighed whatever advantage she would gain by staying home and fighting for her health. She insisted to the end that she was doing everything right, and she sincerely believed it.

Janet struggled on for another 18 months. She managed to control her diabetes quite well and protected her kidneys to some extent. But her heart grew weaker. One day her husband found her sitting in her favorite chair at home. She'd died of a heart attack.

Janet had become a dear friend, and I grieved for her, as did her family. It was a comfort to know she'd enjoyed the time she had and was ready to go. Would better attention to her health have prevented some of this damage? Probably. But we can always look back and say "if only." Thank God He accepts us as we are, where we are.

---

*See Section 6, Story 5.

STORY 5:

Tackling Diabetic Neuropathy
by Kate Miller, R.N. (pseudonym)

I am a 58-year-old registered nurse and have taught nursing, so I should have known better. Actually, I did. But I didn't take my problems seriously. I cooked things I liked with lots of butter, dairy products, eggs, and chicken. I also continued eating plenty of pork and drinking lots of beer. *I'll do better next week,* I kept telling myself.

I had plenty of warning. I'd been overweight for several years and was still gaining. I had developed hypertension 12 years before and attempted to control it with medication. Next came diabetes, and for nearly 10 years I've treated it with oral insulin. My feet and legs developed tingly and "crawly" sensations and began feeling numb. Then the pains began and kept getting worse.

Finally I had to take Empirin with codeine in order to sleep at night. The bottoms of my feet felt as though they were sunburned all the time. I had several episodes of gout [a very painful type of arthritis] that caused my big toe joint to become red and swollen, making me feel even more miserable.

The day came when I could not walk, even in the softest slippers and on the softest carpet. It felt as though I was stepping on razor blades. I finally got serious and signed into a NEWSTART program. During my first few days I could hardly make it around the flagpole. But my distance increased with time. My weight went down, and my blood pressure normalized without any medication. I learned how to keep my blood sugar within normal levels with small doses of insulin.

But the most amazing results relate to my diabetic neuropathy, which I'd had for nearly five years. Once diabetes attacks the nerves in the legs and feet, they rarely recover. But my feet did. Not only were Weimar physicians impressed, but so were several visiting doctors. I was told that it is very unusual for diabetic neuropathy to reverse itself the way my feet have. It's a miracle! I thank God for it.

Author's Note: Dr. Milton Crane, a research scientist working with Weimar Institute, has treated quite a few NEWSTART patients with diabetic neuropathy, with encouraging results. He is following these people carefully to determine how long their improvement continues and how much it relates to their ability to control the disease once they get home.

STORY 6:

Intensive Care Did It

My doctor kept urging me to go to a NEWSTART program, but I couldn't face it," Eve Humphrey told me. "I'm a real homebody and knew I'd be desperately homesick. So I tried to do it at home." Eve gave me a shy, self-conscious smile. She was a gentle, motherly kind of woman. "Anyway, I started out on a 600-calorie diet. I was badly overweight, and in spite of 50 units of insulin a day my blood sugar hovered around 400. I stayed on the diet for two weeks, starving all the time. Finally I couldn't stand it and began eating again.

"The day after Thanksgiving I had a severe attack of angina. I took several nitroglycerin tablets, but they didn't help. My doctor sent me to the hospital, and I was in intensive care for three days. They said it wasn't a heart attack, but it was a close call. They told me if I didn't get my weight and blood sugar down, I would have one for sure. That did it! So here I am."

Noting how uneasy she felt in this new place, I took her around to meet our staff members and several of the patients who would be in her class. Feeling their warmth and friendliness, she finally told her husband that he could go home—she would stay.

Three weeks later the scene in my office had changed considerably. No longer shy and self-conscious, Eve was more like a fountain ready to bubble over.

"I can't believe what's happening! I'm steadily losing weight on my 800-calorie diet, and I haven't felt hungry at all. My blood sugar is nearly down to normal with only 20 units of insulin. If I continue to lose weight, they tell me there is hope I may be able to control my diabetes by the diet alone. My tiredness is gone, and I'm walking a half mile two to three times a day, with only occasional slight pain. I'm not sure I fully understand how you do it, but it really works."

My teacher instincts jumped into action. "Remember the lecture on carbohydrates and fiber? The plant food diet you have been eating is so full of fiber, some of which absorbs water and swells up in your stomach, that you feel full and satisfied after each meal, even on a much smaller number of calories.

"But that isn't all. The fiber, as it travels through the intestines, slows down and evens out the absorption of food into the bloodstream. This helps stabilize your blood sugar and your energy level."

"Is that why you don't feed us refined foods and animal products, because they have little or no fiber?" Eve questioned.

"That's one good reason. Another is that most of those foods contain excessive amounts of fat and cholesterol, two of the substances that help build plaque in your heart arteries and cause you to have angina."

"That's a relief," she said with a happy sigh. "One diet does it all—helps me lose weight, controls my diabetes, and protects my heart arteries."

"Don't forget the exercise," I reminded her in parting. "Exercise is the key to making it all work."

STORY 7:

A Matter of Choice: My Personal Testimony

I stiffened as the needle punctured my vein. Feeling like a martyr, I was serving as my own guinea pig. The experiment was under way. After obtaining my fasting blood sugar reading (a healthy 80 mg/% [2.1 mmol/l], well within the normal range of 70 to 115 mg/%), I went to an International House of Pancakes for a typical American breakfast. This was my order:

1 glass of orange juice (large)
3 large pancakes with butter and blueberry syrup
1 serving of hash brown potatoes
1 Danish pastry
1 cup of decaffeinated coffee with cream and sugar

Feeling Fit

An hour later I faced the needle again, this time for the first postprandial (after-meal) test. The readout of 195 mg/% [5.0 mmol/l] raised my eyebrows, since anything above 185 mg/% [4.8 mmol/l] suggests diabetes. What would the two-hour glucose test tell me? Hopefully, it would be a normal 140 [3.6] or less. When the result came back, it shook me up. At 198 [5.1], I tested unquestionably diabetic! Upset, I requested a three-hour test (not usually done). It was 150 [3.9]. Still diabetic.

Twenty-five years before, I had wondered about my chances of developing diabetes, since it ran in my family. In their later years my father, an aunt, and an uncle, all somewhat overweight, had developed diabetes. A glucose tolerance test at that time identified me as a borderline diabetic with reactive hypoglycemia. I was told to eat six small meals a day.

I was not a snacker and could not face this many meals, so I settled for faithfully eating three meals a day, using lots of fresh and unrefined foods. Desserts were once-a-week specials, and I continued my lifelong vegetarian habits. I kept my weight under tight control, despite several pregnancies. And I checked my fasting blood sugar regularly. For 25 years it remained within normal ranges.

So why did I test so badly on this particular day? I had expected some rise in my blood sugar with the kind of meal I ate, but I didn't expect it to be that disturbingly high! My experiment, however, had another part. A week later, after a normal fasting blood sugar readout of 86 mg/% [2.2 mmol/l], I had the following meal at home:

> 1½ cups of lentil-celery-potato stew over two slices of whole-wheat bread
>
> 1 cup of cooked carrots
>
> lettuce and tomato salad with half an avocado, sliced

This time my one-hour and two-hour blood sugar readings were 114 and 108 mg/% [2.9 and 2.7], respectively! No trace of diabetes. In fact, the levels did not even exceed the limits for a normal fasting blood sugar. Both sets of blood sugar tests, one week apart, had been done at the Loma Linda University Clinical Laboratory. They were certainly not biased toward me. They had no idea who I was or what I was up to.

For years I had been teaching others about the value of a high-fiber, low-fat, low-refined food diet in normalizing adult-onset diabetes. But now it struck home strongly to see this fact illustrated in such a spectacular way in my own body. Of course, in this experiment I was the only case, and in scientific circles that doesn't carry much weight. However, I have seen the same thing happen, over and over, to Type II (adult-onset) diabetics who are willing to make the necessary lifestyle changes.

It has been impressive to face the prospect that for me being diabetic or not is a matter of choice. And that is both frightening—and exciting!

Have you wondered why people who basically live the same way experience different diseases? Some of us carry the genes of certain hereditary diseases, such as cystic fibrosis, which so far medical science has been unable to prevent. Others of us have what is called a "genetic predisposition" to certain diseases that run in our families. Many people think they can't escape these diseases either, but that's not true.

> **I discovered a genetic predisposition to adult diabetes. By maintaining a normal weight and eating a high-fiber, low-fat diet, I've kept it at bay.**

You've been reading story after story in this book about people who have overcome genetic predispositions to familial diseases by paying attention to lifestyle factors. In the above story, for example, I discovered a genetic predisposition to adult diabetes. But by carefully maintaining a normal weight and eating a high-fiber, low-fat diet, I've kept the disease at bay for 25 years. (I also have a genetic predisposition to obesity, so it hasn't been easy.)

My husband has a genetic predisposition to high blood pressure, which he did develop in midlife. But when he changed his lifestyle (lost 40 pounds, exercised regularly, and limited salt intake), his blood pressure became normal and has remained so for 15 years.

The "Sidestreamers":

NEWSTART Detours

idestream smoke is now a household word. Even children understand that smoke inhaled by those around a smoker can be almost as harmful as smoking itself. In the NEWSTART experience, however, it works the other way around. Many spouses and companions are benefiting as much from the programs as the persons they accompany—and sometimes more.

Added to these are people who did not seek out a formal NEWSTART program, but who discovered the principles in a variety of ways and put them into serious practice. We call these people the "Sidestreamers."

STORY 1:

I Like to Know Why
by Rachel Burton, R.N. (name supplied)

ome time ago someone lent us a set of tapes teaching NEW-START principles. My minister-husband and I, although we were health-minded Adventists, determined to begin an even stricter observance of the diet and health principles than we had followed before.

That was three years ago. I'd like to list some of the rewards we have experienced and enjoyed. My husband, who has been asthmatic since childhood, is now free of the disease. He's also had a lifelong allergy to onions. Now we use them freely in our vegetable dishes. All body odors have practically disappeared. We have each lost 30 pounds. The plaque on our teeth is gone. Our hair is less greasy. There is much less "ring around the collar." And our arthritis condition is much improved.

feeling fit

I'm glad we were finally able to observe a NEWSTART program for ourselves. Now I understand better why we adopted this lifestyle. This helps keep me motivated.

STORY 2:

The Portly Reporter
by Len Langevin

I'm nowhere near the man I used to be. In the past six months I've dropped 40 pounds, taken six inches of "waste" off my waist, and dropped my cholesterol level by 55 (1.1 mmol/l) points. The amazing part is how easy it was to do!

It all started out with a man by the name of Dr. Hans Diehl, an epidemiologist from Loma Linda, California, who came to Creston, British Columbia, with a program called Live With All Your Heart. To my newspaper editor instincts, it sounded like something worth a news story. After all, it isn't every day you have a well-known medical researcher coming to a small town like Creston.

The basic message of Diehl's presentation was that North Americans are a bunch of gluttons who are killing themselves with the good life. Heart disease and cancer are taking a lot of lives, many of which could be saved with a proper diet.

In his first few lectures Diehl managed to captivate his audience. And when the day came for the heart screen test, about 400 people showed up. Whether it was just curiosity or a subconscious desire to get back to a normal weight that prompted me to take the test, I don't know. But I took it, and the results were not pretty. Years of double greaseburgers with cheese had taken their toll. My cholesterol level was 211 mg/% [5.4 mmol/l] (a level below 160 is considered optimal), and my weight was just over 190—rather high for my five-foot-seven-inch frame.

"Dangerous," wrote Dr. Diehl at the bottom of the report.

You don't have to be a genius to agree with him. The results floored me. I knew I was a little heavy, but I don't own a scale, and if someone had asked me to guess my weight, I'd have pegged it between 170 and 175. But 190? What a porker! I was so depressed I went out for a bacon and eggs breakfast—to get me out of the poor mood the test results had put me in. I ate breakfast slowly, because it was going to be the last one of its kind for a long time. That day would be a turning point for me.

Diehl's diet was easy enough to follow. He basically advocates common sense: eat the stuff that's good for you—fruits, vegetables, grains, and nuts.

It took about a week for my desire for the doughnut and my craving for the burger to die, but getting used to snacking on bananas, oranges, and apples wasn't tough. His diet was easy to stick to, because it allowed me to eat as much as I wanted of the right stuff and still lose weight. In the past six months I've eaten more per meal than ever before, but I still managed to bring my weight down to 150 by the time Diehl returned for a six-month checkup on his heart screen participants. And guess what? He didn't recognize me!

"When I met you, even though you were young, you looked so devastated, so—debauched." He paused. "I know newspaper people live on caffeine, cigarettes, and stress. Frankly, I had little hope for you."

"Yes, and we tend to grab hamburgers on the way to a town council meeting and fries on the way home," I added.

> **His diet was easy to stick to, because it allowed me to eat as much as I wanted of the right stuff and still lose weight.**

The most surprising aspect of my success is that I didn't follow Diehl's diet religiously. He advocates total vegetarianism—not even chicken, fish, or dairy products, which also pack on the pounds and cholesterol points. I usually indulged in roast chicken or pizza once a week—mostly as a reward for doing so well during the other six days of the week, but partly because I still kind of missed them.

You can imagine that it's nice not to have 40 extra pounds to pack around, but the mental improvement is something I didn't expect. It begins when people start noticing you're losing weight. Few things are better for morale than people telling you you're looking good. Before you know it, you've traded in the baggy sweatshirt and ill-fitting jeans for dress pants, a shirt, jacket, and tie. Then people really start to notice a difference. Not only are they commenting on the weight loss, but they're impressed with the change in attire. That also tends to pick up one's spirits.

Still, Dr. Diehl has his skeptics, most notably restaurant and butcher shop owners. He doesn't do much for their business. I even asked him if this was some sort of Seventh-day Adventist plot to boost membership, since the church was a sponsor of the program.

As you can imagine, I'm no longer skeptical of the good doctor, and my restaurateur friends with salad bars are still making a fair buck off me. Like many people in Creston, I owe a lot of thanks to the heart study team. They've made me, and others, look and feel a lot better—and probably added a few years to our lives.

STORY 3:

I Brought My Wife
by Ron Hardy (name supplied)

I pretty much forced my wife to come to a NEWSTART program. I decided to stay only to make sure she stuck it out. I knew she needed help, but she hated to admit it. Actually, I wasn't much better off than she was. Three years earlier I had undergone a five-vessel heart bypass. I was also 35 pounds overweight and diabetic. Despite all these problems, I wasn't given any advice by my doctors regarding exercise or diet, nor did I receive any rehabilitation. The literature I read indicated that bypass operations usually lasted two to five years. So I figured that was as much time as I had left. I guess I was as stubborn as my wife. I was very skeptical about the program being of any benefit to me. I had the fatalistic feeling that nothing could change that two- to five-year sentence.

In spite of my skepticism, I was very impressed by Dr. DeVine's first lecture. I knew and respected him because he had gone through much the same experience as I had. He convinced me that this program was for me, too, so I opened my heart and mind to everything I could learn.

That was three years ago. I lost those 35 pounds, and my diabetes is under good control. My back problems cleared up, and I work hard, mostly outdoors, from sunup to sundown. It has now been six years since my heart surgery, and I feel just great. I'm sure I have many productive years ahead. One of my greatest joys is sharing with others the news of this wonderful, health-giving, health-restoring lifestyle.

STORY 4:

We Doubled Our Investment
by Clarence Hilliard, M.D.

Right off I need to admit that I haven't been through a NEW-START program myself, but 12 years ago I did send my wife (see the next story). She had hypertension and headaches, and was overweight. She came home so markedly improved and so enthusiastic about the program that I was easily persuaded to join her in this enlightened lifestyle.

I'd like to state that I'm a firm supporter of this kind of medical practice. In seven months we each lost 35 pounds and hadn't felt so well in years. Actually, I'd known these principles most of my life. I wish I had put them into serious practice long before this.

I tell people that our investment produced a double yield in less than seven months because I benefited as much as my wife did. But that isn't really true. How do you put a dollar value on good health, well-being, zest for life, and a new closeness to the Lord?

Today I'm still among the living and feel quite well. Soon after I retired in 1987, I tried waterskiing in icy cold water and ended up with a heart attack. I refused surgery, however, and just continued my NEWSTART program. I've not been sorry. As the years go by, it's hard sometimes not to get careless, and the weight starts creeping back up. But that gets us back to the NEWSTART basics again. We are still completely sold on this way of life and recommend it to those who value their health.

STORY 5:

The Ripple Effect
by Lavonne Hilliard

It was exciting to return home from my NEWSTART experience and find such an interested and supportive husband! He joined me wholeheartedly and has benefited as much as I have.

But that isn't all. I had a chance to share with the young people's prayer group in our church. Soon NEWSTART tapes were flying around the group. Next they wanted recipes, and 50 cookbooks vanished with requests for more. Then they wanted a meeting to ask questions, and more than 60 people showed up. The interest continues, and many are enjoying not only the health blessings but also the bonus blessings of spiritual growth that seem to be built into this program.

To all you wonderful health workers, you will probably never begin to realize the extent of your influence for good. I want you to know what is happening here, in just one little corner of the world—a part of the "ripple effect" of God's great work in our time.

STORY 6:

I Lost 92 Pounds
by John Silva

Although I was overweight and suffered from arthritis and angina, I felt that my wife's problems were more serious than mine. So she enrolled as a patient and I decided to stay with her as her companion.

We attended lectures, ate the food, and walked the trails together. Soon I noticed that I began to feel better. I was also impressed with the improvement experienced by the other patients. By the end of the program I was convinced that this was the way I wanted to live.

It's often said that you can't teach an old dog new tricks, but at age 74 I can honestly say that the basic lifestyle changes were not hard for me. It's been two and a half years, and I've stuck to the program 99 percent. I lost 92 pounds painlessly, without even trying, and I've stabilized at 160 pounds, which is normal for me. I feel better, healthier, and happier than I have for many years.

So you can see that even though I didn't intend to be an alumnus, the NEWSTART program has changed my life.

Author's Note: For the rest of this story, see Barbara Silva's report, "The Struggle Goes On," Section 8, Story 4.

STORY 7:

My Impossible Dream
by Lynette Horwath

As Lance walked into the kitchen, I noticed the small white paper bag he threw into the trash. Another stop at the bakery, for sure. "Honey?" I began. (I knew better but just couldn't help myself. Hope springs eternal when a woman is determined to change her husband.) "Honey, now that I'm a full-fledged fitness instructor, don't you think people will notice how overweight my husband is?" (I'd appealed to his pride. Certainly this should get his attention!)

He sighed. "Look, Lynette, I've heard enough about my weight." His voice was tired—tired of my endless variations on the same old theme. He turned to face me. "You know, honey," he said evenly, his eyes boring into mine, "if you care that much about what people think, perhaps they're noticing how often you stop at the ice-cream parlor on Main Street. It could tarnish your image of being super-fit and nutrition-aware."

Now he'd hit the red button. My passion was ice cream. I'd been trying (without success) for three years to shed 10 extra pounds. And hot-fudge sundaes and double-scoop cones were not helping. Long-married couples sure know where the sore spots are!

I was silent, but I fumed inside. It wasn't fair. He was 60 pounds overweight and I was only 10. But he was right. If I couldn't lose 10 pounds, why was I harping at him? Still, I consoled myself, I'd made some progress. I was in an exercise program and had stuck with it. I was familiar with several books on nutrition and had learned enough to get our family eating more unrefined grains, fewer processed foods and meats, and less sugar. People in town were beginning to look to me as somewhat of an authority on physical fitness. And I'd just begun this new job with the YMCA.

Yet on this night I faced up to my impossible dream. I might be able to help everyone else in town get fit, but I could not help my husband. If there is one thing I can say about getting a mate to lose weight, it is this: don't try. You can't do it.

I am a firm believer in fasting and prayer. Realizing that my own methods were failing miserably, I turned Lance's physical condition over to the Lord. I fasted and prayed on a regular basis, asking God to somehow work a change in my husband's attitude.

Some time after beginning my job as a fitness instructor, I joined a vegetarian cooking class. The more I learned, the more I felt convicted that our family needed further changes in eating habits. But how far could I get with a husband and a teenager who were unhappy over the few changes I'd already made?

About this time my husband experienced some chest pains and went to his doctor for a checkup. After a physical exam and an electrocardiogram, the doctor told him his heart was good and his blood pressure was only slightly elevated. Lance came home almost gloating. I was furious. Couldn't the doctor see that this middle-aged, sedentary, overweight man was headed for disaster? He could have at least warned him about the dangers of obesity.

> It wasn't fair. He was 60 pounds overweight and I was only 10. . . . I might be able to help everyone in town, but I could not help my husband.

The picture changed a few days later on the follow-up visit. Lance's cholesterol was a dangerously high 300 mg/% [7/8 mmol/l]! The doctor explained that he was at high risk for either a heart attack or a stroke. A heart attack didn't seem to scare Lance. But the prospect of a stroke followed by life as an invalid jolted him out of his complacency.

The doctor wanted to put Lance on medication at once to bring down his cholesterol. But Lance remembered my telling him about lowering cholesterol through diet, something I was learning in my vegetarian cooking classes. Besides, as a family we had always been committed to avoiding medications if possible, believing that natural remedies and living through minor pains and sicknesses were in the best interests of the body.

Lance asked the doctor if he could try reducing his cholesterol by diet. The doctor was skeptical, warning him that dietary changes must be made for the rest of his life, which would be extremely difficult. Besides, he said, results with diet alone weren't too good. However, he finally gave Lance a diet.

"Try it for three months," he said. "If it doesn't work, we'll use the medications."

The same neighbor who had invited me to the cooking classes had loaned me a book entitled *To Your Health,* by a Dr. Diehl. When Lance got home from the doctor's office, he noticed the book on our kitchen table and took it with him to work the next day. He came home very excited. "Lynette, I'm convinced," he said. "We've got to follow the suggestions in this book." He was smiling, but I could see that he meant it. "And please buy the neighbor another copy. I'm not parting with this one."

We pulled out the diet the doctor had given to see how it matched up with the guidelines in the book. The book aimed at reducing the fat intake to less than 20 percent, rather than the usual 40 percent. We both had to laugh. The doctor's diet contained 34 percent of its calories as fat. No wonder he was having such dismal results in helping patients get their cholesterol levels down with diet. Lance took it as his personnel challenge to demonstrate to the doctor what a proper diet could really do.

We immediately began increasing our complex carbohydrate consumption of grains and legumes, fruits and vegetables. We removed meats and almost all dairy products from our diet. We followed the suggestions in the book. And we experimented with new foods and recipes. My prayers were being answered. The motivation I could not transfer to my husband was now welling up inside him. My excitement grew as I witnessed his change in attitude and his growing enthusiasm for our new lifestyle.

The three months sped by. Although Lance did not attempt to limit his calorie intake, he lost 17 pounds. My 10 extra pounds dropped off as well. But the best news was the laboratory results. Lance's cholesterol had dropped from 300 to 218 [7.8 to 5.6] ! He could hardly wait to show his doctor. He didn't get to gloat, however, because rather than seeing him, the doctor instructed his nurse to phone Lance with his test results. The nurse explained that his cholesterol was "normal" now, and he would not need to see the doctor for a while. Lance told the nurse that he planned to keep working on his cholesterol until it came down to around 150 mg/% [3.9 mmol/l].

"Well, that is very low," she told him.

"Honey," Lance said to me, chuckling, "I think we need to send a copy of our book to the doctor's office. They are a bit behind the times."

I could hardly believe what had happened. A vegetarian cooking class, a health book, a skeptical family doctor—simple things brought together in God's own special way to soften a heart and to change an attitude. All to make my "impossible dream" come true!

After a number of months, we are still excited about our new lifestyle and our blessings continue. Here are a few of them:

• Lance has been walking two hours a day, regularly. His goal now is to enter a marathon walk.

• My weight has remained stable at my ideal level, and my cholesterol is down to 170 mg/% [4.4 mmol/l]. I'm truly fit now to be a fitness instructor.

• I've expanded my teaching concepts. As my YMCA aerobics class gets out the mats for floor work, I share "Lynette's Wellness Tips" with them. Donning either a nurse's cap or a chef's hat, I give them brief suggestions on how to become the healthy persons they have always wanted to be.

Just last night a friend called. "Thanks, Lynette, for your wellness tips," she said. "Since I began your program I have lost 35 pounds, and my cholesterol has dropped from 263 to 167 [6.7 to 4.3]. My doctor is really happy. How can I thank you enough?"

Legalized Drug Addiction:

Go Now—Pay Later

If one doctor doesn't produce the desired prescription, patients often seek another who will.—A frustrated physician.

Are antianxiety drugs medicine at all? Do they treat any-thing? Or have we doctors helped the pharmaceutical houses promote the biggest binge in history?—Colter Rule, M.D., Chemical addiction specialist.

In today's fast-paced life, people often feel so pressured and stressed, so full of pain and disappointment and hopelessness, that they become increasingly willing to gamble their health—and even their lives—on almost anything that promises relief, no matter how temporary.

For every skid row bum, there are scores of closet alcoholics. And for every street punk looking for a hit, there are many "re-spectable" people numbing their pain with prescription drugs.

The media is full of stories about crack, cocaine, and alcohol abuses. But the widespread use and substantial abuse of an-tianxiety agents and sedatives are largely ignored.

STORY 1:

I Didn't Know I Was Hooked

I would lose one third to one half of my patients if I didn't prescribe Valium or similar drugs.—A family practice physician.

By the third day Avis Stone was ready to share her secret. She had entered our health center with the common complaints of middle age: overweight, stress, hypertension, and depression.

"I started taking tranquilizers 16 years ago," she said in her

181

calm, direct way. "It was a temporary measure to help me cope with a difficult time—a new marriage, teenage stepchildren, starting a business, and learning to keep books. The pills calmed me down and helped me maintain control. I planned to stop taking them when the worst was over. No way would I become dependent on pills! The trouble was that the problems never stopped. Around every corner another crisis threw me off balance.

"As one year stretched into another, I looked vainly for that hiatus of time I needed to get off the medicine. I just seemed too pressured to face the stress and strain of quitting. I kept putting it off. I switched from one kind to another, determined not to get hooked. And I never took very many—one or two a day, sometimes three, occasionally one at night.

"Incredibly, 16 years slipped by. By then my weight had increased, my blood pressure was up, and the stresses and pressures of life were depleting my nervous system. I knew I had to do something. My husband had gone through a NEWSTART program several months before, and he came home so markedly improved that I determined to go there myself.

"When I came here, I still wanted to stop the tranquilizers, but felt that my other health problems were more serious. During my comprehensive health evaluation no one bothered me about the pills. I was glad, actually, because I wasn't ready to part with them. Deep down I was afraid to stop, afraid of how my body would react, and fearful of what might happen to my heart."

I leaned back and smiled at her. "So why are you telling me all this? Have you changed your mind?"

She blushed slightly. "I guess the real reason I'm here is because I ran out of pills." She had to smile at the irony of the situation. "But yes, I do want to stop. I wanted to ask you if you thought it was safe to quit cold turkey." She was serious now.

"I don't think you'll ever have a better opportunity." I said slowly, measuring her reaction. "You are surrounded with caring, supportive people who are eager to help you get well. Highly trained doctors and nurses are available around the clock."

"Yes, yes, I know," she responded. "Besides that, my three days on your NEWSTART program, away from TV, radio, and jangling phones, have calmed my nervous system. The outdoor exercise, the water treatments, and the simple food have relaxed me. Yes, I believe I'm ready for the challenge." She smiled again, but shadows of fear lurked in her eyes.

We knelt together and asked God's blessing on her decision.

Go Now—Pay Later

Avis slept the first night, but the second night she didn't sleep at all, not one wink. Spells of nausea washed over her. She sipped hot water for relief. The next day she began hallucinating. Every time she closed her eyes, she seemed to be looking at water, either swirling around like a whirlpool or rippling and bubbling around her like a stream.

"I would study the scenes intently, observing the details, trying to absorb the meaning," she told me.

"That sounds like a phenomenon some people experience with LSD," I observed.

The hallucinations continued to come and go for seven more days, yet she showed no fear, nor did she complain. She remained calm and rational, able to attend classes and follow her regular schedule. She slept only two or three hours each night for the next few nights, yet she awoke refreshed and did not tire during the day. Sometimes she heard a dull roaring and felt a sense of pressure, like a tight cap on her head. She coped by drinking water and going out to walk. We encouraged her and prayed with her and for her. During the second week she slept better. At the end of two weeks she slept nine hours straight and three hours the next day. After that her sleep pattern normalized.

> **I didn't realize I was addicted to tranquilizers. People kept assuring me they were safe, and I wanted to believe them.**

During the two weeks of withdrawal Avis talked and talked and talked, like the proverbial dike that began with a small leak and grew to a torrent. She had spells of feeling stiff and tight. Intensive hydrotherapy and physical therapy gradually helped her overcome the rigidity, and gradually her muscles let go.

"You are now seeing the *real* Avis," she announced midway through the third week. "She hasn't been around for quite a while." A pair of alert eyes and an excited smile witnessed to her words. "No longer am I tied in a tight knot, trying to push myself around each day. It's like a thick layer of bandages has been removed from my body. I am normal, relaxed, and free at last. I feel like a real person again, rejoining the human race."

At our NEWSTART graduation banquet she shared these words with us. "I came here to lose weight, lower my blood pressure, and recover from stress. All these things happened. But something much bigger also took place. I didn't realize I was addicted to tranquilizers. People kept assuring me they were safe, and I wanted to believe them. Tonight I'm thankful to God and to the staff here for my deliverance. I would be totally stupid to go back to those pills, to that dreary, depressing, self-defeating way of life. It scares me to think what those 'harmless pills' actually did to my body and nervous system.

"I'm thankful for a program like NEWSTART that's dedicated to helping people back to the healthful, restful, sane lifestyle God intends for us to have. Now I know from experience that God's gifts are not only health-giving, but restorative (and healing) as well."

Avis's experience took place back when the medical profession was just beginning to realize that tranquilizers were not the harmless panacea they had appeared to be. These medications are now under tighter control by the Federal Drug Administration. Unfortunately, they are still widely abused. They are easily available on the black market, as well as from unscrupulous health professionals.

This story helps to illustrate that there are no totally safe medications. Medications are sometimes necessary, and often lifesaving, but risks must be weighed against benefits. Using medicine as a Band-Aid to cover uncomfortable symptoms can be harmful and dangerous. Yet how many of us will swallow an aspirin for a headache, when rest or a brisk walk would likely remove the cause?

STORY 2:

The Crack in the Door

Nearly 20 million Americans are using antianxiety drugs, on and off, for short periods, and nearly 3 million are chronic users.—National Institute of Mental Health.

Wanda (not her real name) arrived at our health center with smiles and hugs for everyone. "I'm so glad to be here," she chirped. "I love this place already." She willingly produced several kinds of medication, telling everyone she was anxious to get them out of her life.

Go Now—Pay Later

Wanda was a drug addict—not to the bad stuff, but to the kinds of medicines her various doctors gave her. She needed them to sleep, to wake up, to calm her anxiety, and to combat depression. She didn't believe she had a problem, telling us she had come to NEWSTART to please her family. Like other addicts, she felt sure she could quit whenever she wanted to.

Wanda sailed along the first few days, joking, laughing, and befriending everyone. She was a "people person," warm, witty, and charming. She helped with the sicker patients and ran errands for the nurses. No cloud appeared on her horizon. Perhaps she was right, after all. But our staff felt uneasy. She seemed too high, too ebullient, too eager to impress. But what could we do? This wasn't a prison or a rehab center. We didn't search people or ask them to do anything against their will.

On the fourth day we noticed a change in Wanda. She came into my office, a bit timidly it seemed. "I've just been so impressed by the sincerity I feel in this place," she began. "I've watched the patients struggling with their problems, determined to get well." She tried to smile, but was obviously uncomfortable. "I feel like a phony," she went on, "and I guess that's what I am. I haven't been honest with you. I—I guess I'm too scared."

I reached for her hands and gave them a friendly squeeze. "That's OK," I said. "It's OK to feel scared. We all feel that way when something threatens us."

Wanda took a deep breath, her expression a mixture of apprehension and determination. "I'm ready now to get serious," she said. "I truly want to get well." She opened her purse and placed several medicine bottles on my desk. "This is all of them; I swear it is." She looked at me, checking to see if I believed her, then straightened up. Her voice grew firm. "I want you to promise that no one will give me any of these under any conditions. No matter how much I beg or how hard I cry or what I threaten, don't give them to me."

I assured her we would cooperate. We prayed together, asking God for special strength and blessing.

The next two days were difficult ones for all of us. Wanda couldn't hold still. She became increasingly agitated and paced the halls all that night and all the next day and night. She didn't ask for medicine, but she was constantly moving. We took turns with her, never leaving her alone. She couldn't eat, couldn't rest, and couldn't hold on to an idea. But she didn't complain.

By the third night she began to tire. She went to her room and sat down on the bed. After some warm herb tea, she lay down, and the nurse gave her a massage and prayed with her. When she drifted off to sleep, the nurse turned off the lights and sat in a nearby chair.

Around 1:00 a.m. Wanda suddenly sat up. "Let me out of here!" she demanded in a deep, guttural voice. "Let me out," she rasped again as she jumped out of bed and began throwing herself about the room, crashing into one wall and then another.

Unable to control her, the nurse went for help. Wanda followed her out the door and raced down the hall with a loud, piercing shriek. Everyone in the lodge woke up, and it took four grown men to restrain her. Prayers flew upward as we tried to calm her. She finally relaxed and became quiet. The nurse read to her from the Bible until she finally slept.

The next day she awoke confused and disoriented, and we realized she needed more care than NEWSTART could offer. She was calm and compliant as we took her to a nearby hospital. By the following morning Wanda was herself again. In fact, her husband reported that she was clearer and more lucid than she'd been for months. At the end of the week her grateful family took her home from the hospital, praising God for her restoration.

Wanda had been depending on medications for years, not so much for healing as for help in controlling her mind and her nervous system.

The physicians at the hospital blamed the reaction on a too-rapid withdrawal from her medication. I'm sure that was the explanation for her confusion and disorientation. But those of us present at the health center that night talked about the incident for days. That deep, guttural voice. That eerie, unearthly shriek. Her supernatural strength. Many wondered if it was an incidence of demon possession.

The experience left a deep impression on our entire staff. We knew Wanda was a committed Christian. We knew we had all been praying for her from the moment she arrived. Was it still possible for the devil to get access to her, as indeed it seemed? Wanda had been depending on medications for years, not so much for healing as for help in controlling her mind and her nervous system. Was that the crack in the door that the devil needed? It was a sobering thought.

STORY 3:

I Was a Coffee Addict
by Betty Simi

Nine out of 10 North Americans take a psychotropic (mind-stimulating) drug daily. The culprit? Everyday, ordinary over-the-counter caffeine.

Along with almost everyone else, I didn't believe coffee was addictive. But most coffee contains caffeine, and, like other mood-enhancing drugs, caffeine quietly sinks its tentacles into many of our bodies.

When I joined a live-in NEWSTART program, my first battle entailed trying to quit coffee. The first five days were some of the most miserable of my life. My head ached incessantly. I was too nauseated to eat. Then I was too weak to walk. Twice I was at the end of my endurance and ready to go home. But I was urged to hang on a little longer. On the fifth day I started to pack, but by lunch the symptoms cleared and I started feeling really good.

I had no idea that coffee could do this to a person. How I had longed for just one cup! But I was glad I was allowed to suffer. The experience is indelibly etched in my memory. Whenever I smell it, whenever I feel the tiniest temptation, the memories come flooding back, and I won't touch it. This is the best kind of affirmative action.

Author's Note: Not everyone experiences as difficult a withdrawal as Betty did. But nearly everyone suffers some degree of headache and lassitude the first few days after quitting caffeinated drinks.

STORY 4:

The Whole Truth

Don't expect me to tell you the truth about myself," Diane (not her real name) said as she plopped down into her chair. "I've been to so many doctors, so many psychiatrists, so many hospitals—I'm just sick and tired of the whole thing. Nothing helps

187

anyway." She sighed deeply with exaggerated weariness.

She meant to surprise me, and she did. I'd met her pharmacist-husband a few weeks before, and he'd asked me to help his wife. "It depends on how she feels about it," I had told him.

Diane came willingly enough, checking in for the full 26-day NEWSTART program.

"What am I supposed to do with you if you aren't going to tell me what's wrong?" I said lightly. "Shall I start guessing?"

She suppressed a chuckle. "No problem," she said amicably. "I'm depressed. Isn't every woman my age depressed?"

I had to admit it was a common problem, especially around middle age. "OK, we've got the diagnosis. What we need now is the cause."

"That's what I'm tired of." She sighed her long sigh again. "Digging, digging, always digging for a cause. There are many causes."

"Like what? Kids? Husband? Home? Friends? Church?"

"Yes, all of those." She sighed again. "That's why I never get anywhere with treatment. Nobody can solve all those problems."

> **It was time to lay out her program. Physical exercise is one of the most effective treatments for depression—all kinds of depression.**

I looked to see if she was serious. She was. "Has, uh, anyone suggested the problem might be you?"

"Oh, yes," she said, forcing a little laugh. "I've tried about every antidepressant and tranquilizer there is. I've even had electric shock treatments."

I decided not to question her further. It was time to lay out her program. Physical exercise is one of the most effective treatments for depression—all kinds of depression. Diane needed plenty of exercise. Structure is another important ingredient. She loved gardening and soon took over the care of the plants and flowers around the center. Diane also needed people, and she made many new friends.

Diane was an attractive, warm, loving, and lovable woman. Because we spent considerable time together, we became good friends. And despite her initial reluctance, her story gradually came out. She grew up in an Adventist family, went to Adventist schools, and married an Adventist man. They reared several Adventist children. Diane was a tireless church worker. When the children were older, she resumed her teaching career. "Sounds like an almost perfect life, doesn't it?" she said a bit wistfully. "And I acted the part. My friends often confided that they wished their families were as together as ours.

"The problems began with my feelings about my husband. He is a good man, a good provider, a good father—but so dull, so boring, so predictable. I longed for some fun, excitement, passion—you know, things I thought every other couple had."

Diane stopped and studied the carpet. It was an effort to continue. "I probably don't need to tell you what happened next. Yes, I was tempted into an affair, with a fellow teacher. It was unreal. Together we experienced all those things we were missing at home. It seemed like heaven! We thought we had finally discovered what love was all about."

"And then?"

"The old story," she went on. "The excitement began to wear off and the guilt piled up. The double life, the sneaking around, the disloyalty, and the sin began to crush us. We ended the affair and set about straightening out our lives. But going back was harder, much harder, than I'd ever imagined. I had neglected my home relationships, as well as my spiritual relationships. I had nowhere to turn, no one to comfort me. Instead of becoming more loving to my husband, I became resentful. The contrasts haunted me. I understand now the wisdom of saving the sexual relationship for one's marriage partner. That way you build on what you have together and don't torture yourself with comparisons and unfair expectations."

"What about your relationship with the Lord? Did you feel you'd sinned away your right to heaven?"

"I guess that's what happened. I spent hours with the Bible and other inspirational books. But my prayers seemed to mock me. I felt alienated, lonely, cast out. I became deeply depressed."

"Did you seek counseling? Wasn't there anyone you could talk to?"

"Whom could I talk to? Whom could I trust? You know how treacherous some of the 'brethren' can be. If a juicy tale like that got out . . ." Diane shuddered. "Maybe God can forgive any sin, but there are certain sins the Adventist Church can't ever seem to forgive or forget."

"So you turned all the pain and guilt inward and sealed it up tightly. No wonder you are depressed."

"It's worse than that, I'm sorry to say. This is the part I haven't told anyone. Perhaps it's the reason I can't get well. After a while I felt God wasn't going to help me, that it was up to me. I could think of only two solutions: suicide, or—or . . ."

"Or what? Murder your husband?"

Diane had to smile. It broke the tension. It made what she was going to say next seem less horrible. "No, I hadn't thought of that. But my husband is a pharmacist. I knew where he kept the narcotics. I'd wait until he was asleep, then slip out with his keys and—and help myself."

"Did you become addicted?" I was concerned now. This was an unexpected twist from a woman like Diane.

"Yes and no. I don't think I got seriously addicted physically, at first anyway. I'd take only enough to pull me out of the depression, to make me feel good again. It worked, too. Sometimes I'd get so happy my husband would feel my head to make sure I wasn't delirious with fever! You know the rest—the old story again. I began to need bigger doses more often, just to keep an even keel. Then I'd get scared and quit everything. And of course I'd get sick, throw up, and get so depressed I'd want to die. That's when I'd land in the hospital—again and again." There was no light in Diane's eyes now, no laughter in her voice. She looked so woebegone it tore at my heart.

> **"My husband is a pharmacist. I knew where he kept the narcotics. I'd wait until he was asleep, then slip out with his keys and—and help myself."**

"Dear, dear Diane. You have been trying to carry a double load—an impossible load— all by yourself. Your problem is with God, not with drugs or your husband!"

The tears began to flow. "I think you are right," she sobbed. "I just feel so dirty, so weak, so sinful. And God seems so harsh, so judgmental. If He really cares, why does He let me suffer like this? It's as though I'm on an endless merry-go-round, and I can't get off." She was crying now. I put my arms around her until the storm subsided. She wiped her eyes and tried to smile. "Yes . . . if I could just feel . . . loved . . . forgiven, it would make . . . such a difference. Maybe I need to stop demanding . . . and start . . . listening to God."

Go Now—Pay Later

I opened my Bible and read some of the promises that had made a difference in my life. "Commit thy way unto the Lord; trust also in him; and he shall bring it to pass. . . . Rest in the Lord, and wait patiently for him" (Ps. 37:5-7). We prayed together and hugged each other for a long time.

We helped Diane find a Christian counselor. Away from the pressures and stresses of home, Diane responded rapidly to the love, prayers, and encouragement that surrounded her. At the end of the program, she returned home, feeling stronger and at peace with the Lord.

Diane and I have talked on the phone, exchanged letters, and occasionally gotten together in the years since. She assures me that all is well, but I worry. First, because women who have trouble loving their fathers or their husbands have a harder time accepting the unconditional love of God. And second, because, well, as someone has said, "it is almost impossible not to return to a pleasure once enjoyed." Just ask anyone who has experienced the "pleasure" of alcohol, narcotics, or any other kind of mind-altering drug. The crises in Diane's life did not end at our center. When the going gets really tough and Diane looks at those keys, will the temptation be overwhelming?

Jesus mentions forgiving 70 times seven. Addicts, especially, may need those 490 times. But God is patient. "This is the victory that has overcome the world, even our faith" (1 John 5:4, NIV).

NEWSTART and Arthritis:

The Disease With a Thousand "Cures"

Because arthritis is a chronic disease that never quite seems to go away, even with good medical treatment, hundreds of "folk remedies" have grown up around it. And there are hundreds more unproven, expensive, and often outright quack treatments offered to vulnerable arthritis sufferers by unscrupulous promoters.

Arthritis is a general term for diseases of the joints. There are many kinds of arthritis, but we will look at only two of them. *Osteoarthritis* is the most common type and usually occurs when a joint's blood supply becomes inadequate. Just as a heart will weaken and ultimately fail when the coronary arteries clog up with plaque, so joints begin to break down when the arteries supplying them become narrowed or obstructed. For this reason, most osteoarthritis responds to NEWSTART principles, because lowering the fat in the bloodstream improves circulation, as do exercise and hydrotherapy. Since joint damage recovers very slowly, short-term improvement is rarely dramatic. As time goes by, however, many people have experienced remarkable remissions, as did Ina Canaday, whose story is included in this section.

Rheumatoid arthritis, on the other hand, results from inflammation of the joints (redness, swelling, pain, fever, etc.), rather than from injury or wear and tear. Rheumatoid arthritis is an autoimmune disease, related to asthma, hay fever, and other types of disease that have an allergic component. NEWSTART principles have been most effective against this disease with those patients who are willing to adopt a very strict vegan diet (no animal products at all). This is not so surprising, since milk is a common cause of food allergies, with eggs and beef close behind. Studies have shown, for example, that more than 100 antigens (perpetuators of allergies) may be released during the digestion of cow's milk.

In the following stories both Mary and Clara have been in remission from the disease for many years. Both have been strict vegans.

STORY 1:

Sixty Pills and a Wheelchair

Mary Ross was another legend around Weimar Institute. I finally caught up with her in 1981, when she told me her story.

"Yes, it's true," Mary assured me. "I was taking 60 pills a day and needed a wheelchair when I came to Weimar's first NEW-START class in 1978. I couldn't raise my arms. I couldn't comb my hair. I couldn't climb stairs. I was nearly bedridden with advanced rheumatoid arthritis. Besides that, I had hypoglycemia. I carried snacks everywhere, even to church, to ward off the shakes and the disorientation that would follow. I was also overweight. A recent stroke blurred my vision, caused me to stagger, and made me feel dizzy and nauseated. When I walked, the landscape around me seemed to whirl, and I felt as if the pavement was coming up to hit me in the face. I lived in fear and dread of the next stroke, the big one. I was only 56 years old."

It had been three years since Mary's NEWSTART experience. I asked her what had happened in the interim, wondering how strictly she had been able to maintain the schedule.

"What's happened? It's hard to believe! The hypoglycemia is gone. I've lost 25 pounds and now weigh 120 pounds, ideal for my height. I walk three miles a day with minimal pain and only an occasional mild flare-up of my arthritis. There is no observable residual from my stroke, and I've not had any more strokes. I've taken no pills for three years. In fact, I started to feel better the day after I stopped all those pills."

She said that in the 18 months prior to her NEWSTART program she'd been very ill and had spent thousands of dollars seeking medical help. "I saw eight doctors and collected 60 pills—some were drugs, and some were supplements. I was also taking injections for arthritis, but all the treatments and medicines did was take the edge off the pain. I was advised to start cortisone, but I really feared that medicine. Rheumatoid arthritis is a long-term disease, and I did not want to become addicted. When I left NEWSTART in 1978, I determined to stick to this new lifestyle, and I have.

"Tom and I are very active socially and have lots of company. I cook them big, wonderful gourmet meals so they won't feel deprived because of me. But I don't even taste the food. I have my potato, fresh vegetables, and salad. If I am ever tempted to cheat, I just stop and remind myself of the shape I was in before NEWSTART. No, I haven't cheated. I've stuck with the diet and exercise program faithfully. We travel a lot, and I pack beautiful lunches, full of fresh, wholesome food. When we eat out, I have no trouble getting a baked potato and a fresh salad. I usually bring whole-wheat bread along.

> **"Yes, I'm strict. People just cheat themselves when they don't keep up their good health habits. Most people just want a three-week miracle."**

"Yes, I am strict. People just cheat themselves when they don't keep up their good health habits. Most people just want a three-week miracle at NEWSTART; they don't want to use their willpower. My only real problem is my mother. She continually offers me things I can't eat. She feels threatened when I refuse them. I guess she will never understand."

When I began working on this book, I thought of her. It had been 15 years since I'd heard from her. Was she still around? Was she still OK? Did she still feel loyal to her NEWSTART lifestyle?

Yes, yes, and yes! she wrote. *I've been at least 95 percent faithful to it all these years. I believe with all my heart that if it hadn't been for NEWSTART, I wouldn't be around today. Life is too precious, too important, to take chances with. I have too much to live for, too much to do. Food is in your mouth only a moment, but it can stick around your body for a lifetime. I am 73 years old now, busy, active, and doing fine.*

STORY 2:

Restoration of the Poet

Hiking to the picnic at Bear River, I was trying my best to catch up with 80-year-old Clara Howland. Her face crinkled into a smile as she recognized me.

"Clara . . . would you . . . write a poem . . . about this place . . . this lifestyle?" I was still out of breath. "One I can publish . . . in my magazine?"

"You want to print my poem?" Her voice indicated shock and dismay, but her eyes twinkled. "I'll think about it," she said as we caught up with the rest of the group.

The first time I saw Clara she was reading a poem to a group of NEWSTART alumni at Weimar Institute. This trim, ramrod-straight, smiling woman intrigued me. I had to meet her. I found that Clara wasn't really a poet. She was a schoolteacher of 44 years' experience. And her buoyant health wasn't a genetic gift, either. It was a fairly recent "miracle" for which she thanked God every day.

Gradually her story came out. Despite many serious and determined weight-control efforts, Clara had been markedly overweight since young adulthood. Eventually she developed a serious type of arthritis, with bouts that recurred for the next 30 years. But that didn't stop her. She hung on to her teaching with tenacious dedication. On good days she wrote poems of thanksgiving. On bad days, when the joint pains came, she prayed and endured, never giving in to complaining. Her active mind constantly searched for ways to improve her health.

In April 1978 the disease hit with a vengeance. Every joint swelled, and she hurt so badly she could scarcely move. She was admitted to the hospital for care by a specialist. Stronger pain pills were the only additional treatment offered her at the time. She resisted for four days, but by the fifth day she decided to give them a try. The medication upset her stomach and blocked her intestines, intensifying her misery. Tears trickled down her cheeks, an unusual emotional surrender for this strong, positive woman. In her helplessness she fought a swelling tide of self-pity and prayed for guidance.

After two weeks she left the hospital, no better at all. Friends took her in, because she could not care for herself. As the hours and days crept by, she began thinking about a doctor friend who lived some distance away. He had worked at the Pritikin Longevity Center and was now involved in the development of Weimar Institute's NEWSTART lifestyle program. She decided to call him.

"Please, just tell me what to do and I'll do it," Clara promised him after describing her condition. "I can still use the phone. You can counsel me by telephone."

This doctor laid out a totally different treatment program. He told her to eat only whole plant foods, very simply prepared; to take alternate hot and cold baths in the tub; to drink quarts of water; to take short sunbaths every day; and to exercise her painfully crippled limbs, even ever so little, to maintain range of motion.

Clara's friends helped her carry out the treatment plan as prescribed. It wasn't easy without recipes or instructional books, but they forged ahead. Food trays were filled with fresh fruits and vegetables, with brown rice and whole-wheat bread. Painful joints were exposed to the sun, then gently exercised by degrees, despite the pain. When Clara could get into the bathtub without help, it was cause for celebration. When she could walk a short block, she felt she had the world by the tail!

> **On good days she wrote poems of thanksgiving. On bad days, when the joint pains came, she prayed and endured.**

In three weeks' time she was able to move back to her own home. She continued every detail of the program, resting frequently and gradually decreasing her pain pills. She filled her heart with songs and her mind with praise and gratitude.

Clara continued to get better. Her hypertension disappeared. In July, three months after her hospitalization, she was able to drive her car. By August she could walk a mile. With such impressive results, Clara dedicated herself to sticking with this program for the rest of her life.

Feeling the need for more knowledge, she entered Dr. Charles Thomas' Preventive Health Care Center in Banning, California, that fall. She learned the rationale for her new lifestyle, and she learned how to cook. The hydrotherapy (water) treatments were relaxing and helped leach out the remaining stiffness and pain. Every day she grew stronger. Her zest for life returned, and poems once again began flowing from her pen.

There was a surprise bonus yet in store. Clara had noticed that her clothes were becoming very loose. One day she got on a scale and discovered she'd lost 60 pounds.

"Just like that?" I snapped my fingers.

"It seemed like that—I hadn't tried to lose weight. I was just concentrating on getting well."

She went on with her story: "I continued to lose weight, slowly, and then one day I simply stopped losing. I guess I had reached my proper weight. I lost a total of 95 pounds." Her eyes softened as she looked out over the hills. "You know," she said, "I love this place. Although I have never gone through a NEWSTART program, I have attended the alumni homecoming week each year since I got well."

Some years later I was again at a NEWSTART alumni reunion, and I looked for Clara. There she was, still ramrod-straight, pink-cheeked, trim, and healthy, with eyes that seemed to smile as though remembering a good joke. Eleven years had passed since her recovery, and she was still active and pain-free. She had hiked the six miles to the picnic, where I'd finally caught up with her.

When the picnic ended, Clara climbed into the bus and sat beside me. "I'll write that poem for you tonight," she promised.

"And if it's good enough, I'll publish it," I teased.

It was—and here it is:

THE NEWSTART CURE

Pine trees wave their health-filled branches as we hikers
  stride along.
Flowers scent the air around us, while the wild birds trill
  their song.
People come to find true healing from the lifestyle of NEWSTART,
And so many longtime sufferers find relief and take new heart.
Medications soon are lessened; many of them disappear.
For natural food and exercise are the "drugs" they use up here.
Sunshine, rest, fresh air, and water bring results both safe
  and sure.
Patrons come from all directions to enjoy this God-blessed cure.

The Disease With a Thousand "Cures"

STORY 3:

From Paradise Lost to Paradise Regained

Ina felt good as she and Ivan strode along in the brisk air. The first rays of sunlight were just beginning to spill over the horizon.

"Ivan?" Her voice was tentative. "I . . . I would like to walk 71 miles on my seventy-first birthday." She shot a glance at her good-natured, patient husband, "Do you think I could do it?"

Ivan drew in a quick breath. Less than two years earlier his wife had faced the prospect of being an invalid. He knew what this would mean to her. "Sure, honey, why not?" he encouraged. A tiny smile crept over his face. "Only—well, you know, I'll be 73 in a few weeks. Couldn't we make it 73 miles?"

Ina felt like jumping up and down. They hugged each other. Then they solemnly shook hands and the pact was made. The date was two months away.

There had been a time when Ina felt like a golden girl in her golden years, living out golden dreams. After farming in Washington's Yakima Valley for 35 years, Ivan and Ina Canaday sold out and moved to Belize, Central America. They purchased 50 acres of bush land and built a large, airy two-story house. They cleared, fertilized, and planted their land with luxuriant tropical and semitropical plants and trees. They grew oranges, mangoes, avocados, pineapples, papayas, and cashews.

With a sense of fulfillment they settled in to share their bounty and to teach successful farming methods to the needy people around them. They praised God for helping them find a mission in this little piece of paradise.

But Ina's dream began to unravel. Most of her life she had ignored a recurring, nagging back pain. But despite the sunshine, mild climate, and the easy life in Belize, the pain gradually became too severe to ignore. Simple walking became an agonizing experience. Acute arthritis complicated her back problems, and Ina could barely move. Neither rest nor medication relieved her pain or her swollen joints.

By their seventh year in "paradise," Ina's suffering was so intense that she became seriously depressed and longed to die. A frightened Ivan flew Ina to the States, where she had surgery for a herniated disc in her spine. Her neurosurgeon recommended that they stay in the States, where she could be near good medical care. Although her back felt much better, she was warned that there was no assurance of lasting improvement.

Ivan found a job as assistant farm manager at the Weimar Institute in northern California. Then he and Ina dealt with leaving Belize—their home, their plantation, their friends, their dream. They packed their things and said goodbye. *Paradise Lost* took on new meaning.

Shortly after moving to Weimar, Ina had a physical examination by one of the NEWSTART physicians. "You need exercise," he told her. "I want you to walk two miles every day."

Two miles a day? In her condition? Ina felt that was too big a pill for her to swallow. But Ivan encouraged her and offered to walk with her. It was unbelievably hard. They managed only a half mile the first day, but they kept at it. One morning they covered one mile; a few days later, two. In a few weeks they were walking four miles a day. In time, their walks became a habit neither would think of missing.

Ina began to feel better. She showed increasing interest in the institute's multifaceted lifestyle program, which included a healthful, plant-food-centered diet. As her health improved, her natural sparkle and love for life returned. At the end of two years she felt ready to tackle the long birthday walk.

To celebrate our forty-sixth wedding anniversary we hiked to the top of Mount Whitney and back in 14 hours.

The couple carefully mapped out their eight-week training period. Each weekday morning they walked from 4:00 to 6:00. Often they walked again after supper. The first weekend they walked 10 miles; the second, 20. Each weekend they added 10 miles. On the sixth weekend they walked 63 miles. The "73-mile birthday" was 10 days away. They were ready. They felt healthy, strong, and pain-free.

Their personal marathon began at 7:00 p.m. under a full moon. It ended 23 hours later near sunset. Their daughter, Mary Jo Canaday, drove a van beside them and doled out water every 10 miles and food every 20 miles while they stopped for a short rest. Their travel menu included fresh fruits, vegetables, and whole grains.

During their 23-hour walk, the Canadays slept one and a half hours and rested another three hours. Their pace averaged just under four miles an hour.

"The whole purpose of this walk was to call attention to the way that simple lifestyle changes can improve the quality of life, even for older people like us," Ina told reporters. "You just can't get good health sitting around in a rocking chair. Our bodies are designed for exercise and healthy food. What happened to us can happen to other people."

Both Ivan and Ina work full-time—he on the farm, she as tour guide for the hundreds of visitors who come to Weimar Institute annually. They continue to walk six to 10 miles each day on the mountain roads around their home.

Four years after their celebrated birthday walk I wrote to the Canadays, asking how they were getting along. This is what I learned:

Yes, four years have passed since Ivan and I left our tropical paradise, Ina wrote. *But paradise can reappear in unexpected places. We both like our new jobs, and we both have grown to love the cool, clean, alpine air of the Sierras. In 1987 we walked a total of 2,580 miles. To celebrate our forty-sixth wedding anniversary we hiked to the top of Mount Whitney and back in 14 hours. Mount Whitney is 14,494 feet high, the tallest peak in the contiguous United States. I can honestly say we've never felt better. My pain, stiffness, and depression are nearly forgotten memories.*

I know that God led us to this place and to this knowledge. He is eager to bestow on all of His children the delights of abundant health to be found by living in harmony with His principles. For us, Paradise Lost *has become* Paradise Regained. *No material thing can possibly compensate for poor health. We feel rich and blessed beyond our greatest dreams.*

The birthday walk occurred in 1984. The Canadays continued their work at Weimar Institute until 1989, when they moved back to their old homestead in the state of Washington. Ina remembers that in 1983 she could barely walk a half mile, her heartbeat was very irregular, and her back was in bad shape. She marvels still at all the good things that have happened since. "What we learned about NEWSTART and put into practice these past 13 years has made all the difference in the world."

Now 83 years old (1996), she says she feels great most of the time. She is still able to do hard, heavy work. Her walking is more limited these days because Ivan has developed Parkinson's disease. But she and a neighbor woman get out and hike five to 10 miles quite often, especially when the spring wildflowers are in bloom.

WELL, I SEE YOU FELL OFF THE WAGON . . . YOU TESTED POSITIVE FOR CHOCOLATE!
ERJ

Adventist Celebrities:

Older Can Be Better

I've lived some 23 years beyond the life expectancy given me when I was born—and that's a source of great annoyance to a number of people.—Former President Ronald Reagan.

Older *can* be better. So say the Adventists you'll read about in this section who have attracted wide media attention because of their feats of endurance. All were near-invalids at the time most people retire, and all regained their health by simplifying their diets and lifestyles and exercising their bodies.

But they didn't stop at that. Pushing on and on to their physical limits, they reached heights of accomplishment rarely seen in our time.

STORY 1:

Reaching a Little Higher

Death Valley's debilitating heat sucked Richard Kegley's strength as he stepped from the cool desert museum into the 126-degree heat outdoors. He walked to his motor home and sat on the bumper. "What have I gotten myself into?" he mumbled.

His wife took a quick breath but said nothing. She feared for his safety and half hoped he would give up the idea, yet knew how hard they had both worked to reach this moment. Richard was about to begin one of the world's toughest challenges to runners: the Death Valley to Mount Whitney run. The rules required that he run the distance between the lowest and highest points in the contiguous United States during the peak of summer, between July 1 and August 31. His wife and grandchildren would be his support crew.

Feeling Fit

Now it was Saturday, August 1. In a few moments he would begin running in scorching heat at 282 feet below sea level. In the next 146 miles he would climb to 14,494 feet and adjust to near-freezing temperatures. The course had defeated men much younger than he, but right now Richard's concerns were for his support group: his 66-year-old wife, Margaret; his 19-year-old granddaughter, Janelle; and his 16-year-old grandson, Scott. They would be supplying his nourishments and the 39 quarts of water he would drink during the next five days. His wife would soak and massage his feet when he stopped during the heat of the day. Their job would not be easy. Support crews frequently collapsed from heat and exhaustion. If his crew did, his run would be over.

Richard knew that only eight of the 80 people before him who had officially attempted this course during the previous 10 years had finished. And the oldest of the eight had been 20 years younger than he was. He fought his fears as they waited for sundown. At 8:11 the air had cooled to 111 degrees, although the ground temperature remained much higher. His crew was ready. So was he. His wife started the motor home.

> **This was one of the world's toughest challenges to runners: . . . In the next 146 miles Richard would climb 14,494 feet in near-freezing temperatures.**

Here it is, he thought. *The first step, the step that's going to commit me to this ordeal.* It was hot, so very hot. *I can't even breathe—how can I run?* He almost panicked. *Put one foot down, then the next. Again. Again.* Soon he was in rhythm. Scott, who had run with him to help him start, returned to the motor home. Now Richard was alone. The sliver of moon seemed out of place in the oppressive heat. The bats flying nearby dived for his wife's white hair when she sprinted to him with water. He looked up at the stars shimmering beyond the hot air and thought about how he had gotten from a hospital bed 10 years before, clutching an oxygen mask, to this punishing run in Death Valley.

Death Valley, that's what his life had been. Richard had suffered from asthma for years. Even though he carried a small pharmacy with him, he had frequent flare-ups that landed him

204

in the hospital. After his last admission at age 58, he decided he had to do something different. He had a few things going for him. He didn't smoke or drink, and he had been a vegetarian all his life. But in spite of all that clean living, he had put on an extra 50 pounds. And there was that asthma.

He bought an exercise bicycle and began to use it every day. His doctor son prescribed a regimen of walking. Soon he was walking the two miles to his auto dealership. His wife joined him. She had her own problems, having survived a stroke and four heart attacks, as well as being overweight. They cut all refined foods and most sugars and fats from their diet.

Within a month Richard ran a mile. Within a few more months Margaret had dropped 20 pounds and had run her first marathon, placing second in her age group. As Richard's endurance improved, the extra weight disappeared. His asthma faded away and never returned. He began to enjoy life. He felt young again. By this time he and Margaret were both hooked on running. Margaret covered two to four miles, and Richard six to eight miles, five days a week. They both ran marathons.

During the next 10 years Richard ran 25,000 miles. His credits include the Boston Marathon, four Lake Tahoe runs (72 miles each), and four Six-Day Races in San Diego. In the 1984 Six-Day Race he set a new record for men older than 60 by covering 331 miles. But tonight, in the oppressive heat of Death Valley, those distant successes seemed like faded dreams. The cloying heat, the 180-degree ground temperature, the desperate barrenness that gave Death Valley its name, settled upon him and penetrated to the core. But he would keep going. *Put one foot down, then the other, again, again.*

The motor home stalled. Vapor lock. Richard retraced his steps to switch gas tanks. After that, Margaret kept the van ahead of him.

Death Valley held him in its clutches until Monday, the debilitating heat sucking his strength. As he reached the foothills, dysentery set in. His throat was raw. He could barely swallow water, his link to life. He wanted to stop; his body screamed for rest. But deep inside he knew he would not quit. He couldn't. His crew depended on him. *Put one foot down, then the other, again, again.*

The road climbed to 5,000 feet before descending again. Finally he reached Lone Pine, the last town before Whitney Portal. Whitney Portal, the place where the road ended, the place where he would leave his crew, the place where he would be alone.

On Thursday, August 6, Richard left Whitney Portal, 6,500 feet from the mountain's top. The last 11 miles would be his alone. His crew could not come. There was only a trail with switchbacks to the peak. Weakened from dysentery and exposure, Richard knew that if he did not reach the top by 1:30 p.m. his dream could be lost. If he was not back at Whitney Portal by sundown, he feared he would die during the night. The sudden drop in temperature would be lethal to him in his weakened condition.

Doggedly he climbed. *Put one foot down, then the other, again, again. And then again.* The air was getting thin. His head ached. He was nauseated from altitude sickness. He could barely see. The road seemed to disappear. Everywhere he looked were boulders, huge boulders, blocking his way. And then he saw it—the cabin that sits at the peak of Mount Whitney. Weather-scarred, it rose above the boulders. Aching in every fiber of his body, he stood on the summit and squinted at the world. He took pictures, signed the register in the cabin, then turned to go. It was over.

> **Although the Death Valley-Mount Whitney run was his toughest, Richard considered the 46-mile Grand Canyon Double Crossing the most grueling.**

Physically and psychologically spent, he suddenly felt overwhelmingly depressed. He had realized his dream, but there were 11 excruciating miles left. His toes jammed into his shoes. His legs wobbled. His joints throbbed.

And then hikers on the trail came to him. They had heard of his unprecedented feat—at 68, the oldest person ever to complete the Death Valley-Mount Whitney run! They surrounded him, not holding him, but talking, encouraging, praising, morally supporting him. They stayed with him, giving him water, keeping his mind off his pain, until he descended to Whitney Portal. Then he knew he was a victor! But Richard Kegley had been a victor long before this. He had salvaged what had been the wreck of his physical self. He had faced overwhelming odds. And he won. It didn't happen all at once. He took one step, then another, again, again. And he won.

Older Can Be Better

. . .

While admitting that the Death Valley-Mount Whitney run was his toughest, Richard considers Arizona's 46-mile Grand Canyon Double Crossing to be the most grueling, the one he came nearest to failing. "You start at the South Rim, run down to the riverbed, which is a 6,000-foot drop in elevation, then run along the river for a few miles, then up the other side of the canyon to the North Rim," he explains. "It's like experiencing the four seasons in one day. It was spring on the South Rim, summer in the riverbed, fall as I went up the north wall, and winter on the North Rim."

Exhausting enough even to listen to! But this is a *double* crossing. Runners must retrace their path, down from the North Rim, along the canyon bottom, then back up to the South Rim starting line. It was on this last, steep, uphill climb that Richard got into trouble.

"I thought I was finished," he says. "The race rules state that if you drop out on the course you have to pay a $75 fee to be air-lifted out by helicopter. But I knew I could go no farther, so I asked these two race monitors to call in the helicopter. I was really thirsty and asked them for some water. They had a bottle, but they poured almost all of it out onto the ground before handing it to me, leaving only a couple sips in it. I was mad! Then they produced a banana, but they handed me only a small piece and trampled the rest into the dirt. I was so angry I was ready to hit those guys. Instead, I turned around and ran the rest of the way up to the finish line. The anger just powered me up. Well, it turned out that those two race monitors wanted me to get furious. They were trying to get my adrenaline flowing. I hugged them later, at the finish, after I figured out what they had been up to."

At 67 Richard Kegley became the only man over 60 to complete this course.

. . .

What does a person do next after establishing two world records? Although Richard is a competitive person, by this time he and Margaret were running not just to win, not just for health, but because they both loved it. "In fact," Richard observed, "our running years have been the most fun years of our lives."

So this couple cooked up another idea—they would run a

marathon (26.2 miles) on their golden wedding anniversary. Their excitement grew when they discovered the 1992 Portland Marathon was scheduled for the very day of their anniversary.

"We're not running this marathon for a prize," they told their friends, "We're running it for fun and celebration."

On September 27 they were ready. They held hands at the start of the run, and friends and family along the route cheered them on. *Runner's World* and *Portland Marathon* magazines featured their feat, and a large banner congratulated them as they crossed the finish line together and were presented with matching gold medallions as souvenirs of their anniversary run. Margaret was 72, Richard 74.

"It was a dream come true," says Richard. "We renewed our wedding vows and had the time of our lives."

Margaret and Richard, now 76 and 78, respectively, are still running various marathons and 10-kilometer runs every year. "We don't run as much as we used to," Margaret says, "but Richard still runs five or six miles most mornings, and I run three or four times a week. We enjoy running, but our main purpose is to demonstrate what a healthy lifestyle can do for a person." The 100 trophies they've collected testify to their success.

STORY 2:

Canada's Courageous Cyclists

You want to *what?*"

"I'd like to bicycle over the Rocky Mountains," Bob repeated. His voice was calm, casual even. "I have this doctor's appointment in Calgary on Friday. It's only 300 miles. If I start out Monday morning, I'm sure I can make it."

Theresa did a double take on this unbelievable husband of hers. Two years ago he'd quit his job because of a painful, arthritic back. When it got worse, he had to give up doing even small jobs in his home workshop. He was so short of breath that he began driving his 22-year-old jalopy to the mailbox 50 yards away. Friends tried to comfort him. "You've worked hard all your life," they said. "You deserve a soft sofa and a *TV Guide*. You're finally free from the daily grind."

But freedom was no prize when it was coupled with constant

pain. The soft sofa became a prison. Food, TV, cigarettes, and alcohol made up Bob's life, but none of them brought any pleasure. He tried to be cheerful. But he hit bottom the day he helplessly watched others buck, split, and stack his winter firewood. "I haven't one shred of ego left," Bob said. "I really don't think I'll live much longer. I'm already past the age that my father and brother died."

"You're only 66 years old," his wife chided. But she couldn't lift his depression.

A few days later Theresa picked up a flyer in her doctor's office about some health meetings coming to town. The doctor noted her interest and urged her to go. "And be sure to take Bob along. Tell him it's doctor's orders."

Bob didn't need any urging. "Things can't get any worse," he said. They both signed up for the "Live With All Your Heart" seminar and began attending the meetings. The results of their health screen evaluation were a severe jolt. Bob knew he had arthritis, but not that he also had high blood pressure, high cholesterol, and diabetes. Theresa's results were no better. And both were overweight enough to be diagnosed as obese.

Dr. Hans Diehl's message was simple: our diets are killing us. Meat, dairy products, sugar, alcohol, salt, and tobacco—all the so-called good things of life—must be removed from our homes, or we will eat and drink ourselves into early graves. Bob and Theresa learned that rich food and sedentary living contributed to coronary heart disease, stroke, diabetes, hypertension, and osteoarthritis. But along with the bad news was good news: these conditions could be improved, and often reversed, by healthful lifestyle changes.

Hope—this was what the Andersons needed. They willingly, even eagerly, decided to make the recommended changes. "I took the gin and vodka and dumped them down the kitchen sink," says Theresa. "Then I cleaned out the fridge—all the meat, cheese, and butter—I just threw out the works."

In one day meat, eggs, salt, alcohol, junk food, and caffeine disappeared from their house and their lives. Cold turkey. The "haul" filled three large garbage bags and included two standing rib roasts they'd purchased the week before. Bob's 35-year-old cigarette habit, which he'd tried many times to break, ended that night also.

"Sure it was a lot of money out the window," Bob said, "but we figured if we were going to try this thing, we were going to go all the way."

The next day Bob slowly and painfully made his way to the mailbox. The effort exhausted him, but he did not give up. He even joked about it. "I must have been a sight," he said. "I was listing 40 degrees to port. I couldn't stand up straight."

They both began walking every day. One block, then two, three, five, and they were on their way. They enjoyed their new way of eating that included whole-grain cereals and bread, fresh fruit, and lots of vegetables, potatoes, and beans.

By the fourth week of NEWSTART Bob and Theresa decided to go to church. They considered themselves to be Christians, but years of indifference and poor health had led to their dropping out. When their perspectives changed, the Word of God took on new meaning, alive with encouragement and full of promises.

By the fourth month the couple were ready to tackle hills and climb mountains. By the sixth month Bob's back pain disappeared. "They say God can make crooked things straight," he deadpanned. "You can see He did it for me." He now stood straight and walked without a limp.

> **Rich food and sedentary living contribute to coronary heart disease, stroke, diabetes, hypertension, and osteoarthritis. These conditions can be improved, and often reversed.**

Theresa loved to walk, but she sensed a restlessness in her husband. She suspected he yearned for something more exciting. She suggested he talk to their son, Don, who was a bicycle enthusiast. "Am I too old to get back on my bicycle?" Bob asked Don over the telephone.

"Well, Dad, are you 90 yet? The sport is a little risky for those past 90."

A few days later a sleek new 18-speed Schwinn bicycle stood in their driveway. Helmet, cycling gloves, shoes, goggles, and other gear followed. Beginning slowly, Bob worked up to 25 to 40 miles a day, six days a week, getting stronger with every mile. Within a year he had lost 32 excess pounds. His blood pressure, cholesterol, and blood sugar had normalized. He chopped his own wood and spent many happy hours in his workshop doing custom carpenter jobs.

The day came when Bob and Don decided to organize their

own bicycle tour—a rugged trip to the Columbia Icefield. Don was young and fit, but he worried about his 68-year-old father. However, after the first day he stopped worrying. "The guy can really ride," he told his mother. "He keeps right up with all of us young guys."

So Theresa wasn't that surprised when Bob announced he wanted to ride his bicycle to Calgary. The challenge of biking 300 miles over the Rockies excited him. They began to plot their trip. And at 7:00 on Monday morning a shiny bicycle flashed down the Anderson driveway and headed for the mountains. Theresa packed the car with supplies and camping gear, then drove on ahead to a campground and prepared lunch. Bob arrived at 1:15 p.m., grumbling because he'd gone only 67 miles. Didn't the man realize how many of those miles were uphill? Theresa laughed and teased him about needing a higher octane fuel. That night after a hearty supper they lingered around the campfire, savoring the goodness of life.

The second day was lovely. The clouds looked like fluffy white stoles draped around the mountains' shoulders. Autumn splashed its colors lavishly, preparing for the long winter sleep. Then, near the summit of a pass, Bob encountered a huge black bear.

"I turned on my afterburners and shot up that hill so fast I still can't believe it!" he bragged to Theresa later.

After another adventurous day and night, Bob rode into Calgary. He'd ridden 301 miles and crossed the Rocky Mountains in three and a half days. He'd met the challenge. And he didn't even have any sore muscles—only a very sunburned nose.

The next morning, refreshed and fit, Bob was ready for his doctor's appointment.

"What? You came here on a *bicycle?*" his doctor asked in amazement. Everything stopped in the famous eye surgeon's office for the next 20 minutes while he extracted details from Bob and inspected his bicycle. "It's about time we had some good news from this office," the doctor said. "I'm calling the paper." In a few minutes reporters surrounded them, taking pictures and peppering them with questions. "We were always led to believe that martinis and rich foods were the rewards of a life of hard work," Bob told the reporters. "I used to have three eggs and six slices of bacon for breakfast. I'd smoke a couple packs of cigarettes a day, have a couple drinks before dinner, then at bedtime I'd have a huge bowl of peppermint ice cream, topped with a gooey topping. We considered our health problems to be an inevitable part of aging. We wanted to enjoy all the good things we could get, but we felt miserable and weren't having any fun. In fact, at times we wished we could hurry up and die."

"But no more!" Theresa picked up the story. "We are no longer simply enduring retirement. We are living our lives to the hilt! We both have bicycles, and we love life on the road."

As their physical health improved, the couple grew spiritually. "We've been born again," they tell people. "Now we have a purpose, a sense of direction in our lives."

That winter they made an extensive trip through the United States, sharing their experiences with many church groups and on radio and television features. Bob said recently that he shudders to think what would have happened to them had they not gone to that health seminar.

"I've decided that second childhood certainly beats the first," he observes dryly, "because there's no one around to tell you what you can't do."

• • •

It was at the urging of Dr. Sidney Kettner, the Andersons' family doctor, that the Andersons attended the health seminar that changed their lives so profoundly. Dr. Kettner reports that Bob wasn't the only Anderson going downhill two years ago. Theresa also had serious problems. Her blood pressure was 180/120 with medications, and her weight was out of control. She'd been depressed for months, some days not even getting out of bed. Often she thought about death. With his back pain and his restlessness, Bob was no help. Neither one could walk very far, and both used their 22-year-old car for trips as short as to the mailbox, some 50 yards away. Theresa was also mildly diabetic.

After a year of practicing their new lifestyle, Theresa's blood pressure was 120/80 without medication. Her cholesterol dropped to 172, and her diabetes vanished. Her resting pulse went from 90 to 65, and she slept well without medication. This radiant, energetic woman held little resemblance to the woman Dr. Kettner knew before. "Her recovery was as remarkable as her husband's," he says.

Theresa enjoyed her moment of payoff too. The day after she lost her fortieth pound, she found a brand-new Chrysler parked in the driveway. Her husband stood nearby, relishing her squeals of delight. "It's all yours. I'm very proud of you for what you've done."

Older Can Be Better

"I remember Dr. Diehl telling us how much money we'd save with this new lifestyle," Theresa reflected, looking at their new car. "Don't you believe it. So far it's cost us a bundle!" But the pleasure in her voice belied any regrets.

• • •

After his record-breaking bicycle ride over the Rocky Mountains, Bob and Theresa began planning a trans-Canada trip. One year later it became a reality.

In order to maximize their effectiveness in promoting good health, Bob and Theresa timed their arrival to coincide with the opening of Dr. Diehl's Ottawa Coronary Health Improvement Project, a four-week seminar similar to the one the Andersons had attended in Creston three years earlier.

In nearly every town along their 3,000-mile route, the Andersons were met, photographed, and interviewed by the media. On their arrival in Ottawa, Perrin Beatty, Canada's minister of health at that time, presented them with a plaque commemorating the event. It read: *To Bob and Theresa Anderson, with thanks for your visit and with every good wish for your continued good health.*

After a year of practicing their new lifestyle, Theresa's blood pressure was 120/80 without medication. Her cholesterol dropped to 172.

Newspaper headlines in Ottawa and across a good part of Canada screamed, *Heart Disease Cyclist Completes Ride of His Life!* One account read, *A triumphant Bob Anderson arrived on Capital Hill in Ottawa after completing a 3,000-mile, 60-day bicycle odyssey from his home in Creston, British Columbia. His ride, promoting good health, would have been impossible three years ago. Anderson, now 69, could then barely walk to his mailbox because of medical problems, including arthritis, diabetes, hypertension, and obesity.*

But his participation in Dr. Diehl's Creston Heart Project changed his life. On his most recent stress EKG test, his cardiologist pronounced him as having the coronary health of a 40-year-old man.

Feeling Fit

• • •

Author's Note: Bob is now 77 and Theresa is 71. I recently met their physician, Dr. Kettner at a medical meeting. "So how are the Andersons?" I wanted to know.

"Well, Bob is busy right now building my new house," the doctor told me. It was apparent that the couple were doing just fine!

STORY 3:

The Incredible Hiking Hulda

Newspaper headlines around the world reported her triumphs. Reporters from television, radio stations, and newspapers vied for interviews and took pictures. Her telephone rang and rang.

Who was this media darling of the late 1980s? A quiet, gentle, old woman named Hulda Crooks. Barely five feet tall, with hair like a puff of snow, this woman became the best-known and most publicized Seventh-day Adventist in recent history, all because of her unique quest for health.

How did it happen? Very slowly, actually. Hardly anyone had ever heard of her until she started climbing Mount Whitney at age 66. She kept climbing this tallest peak in the lower United States every year for the next 25 years. She reached the top 23 times and was prevented from completing the hike only twice, because of severe weather and poor trail conditions.

Hulda did not start life as a robust child. She recalls those early days and admits to problems with overeating. "I'd eat chocolate until I threw up, and then I'd eat some more. My brother told me I was going to be as wide as I was tall."

Instead, she became a Seventh-day Adventist and adopted the vegetarian lifestyle advocated by her church. She married, had a son, kept house, tended her garden, her flowers, and her animals. Her life might have continued in peaceful anonymity except that before she was 65 she had lost her husband and her only child.

Alone and lonely, she longed for a challenge, for a way to share her faith. She loved mountains and had often dreamed of climbing some of the great peaks. So she began walking. As her strength increased, so did her adventures. At a time when most women are relaxing into comfortable retirement, Hulda began conquering mountains.

• • •

I met Hulda Crooks in 1986, when she was 90 years old. She told me that several months before her yearly Whitney climb she teasingly challenged Jerry Lewis of California's Thirty-fifth District to "climb the mountain with me next time." She did it in fun, never dreaming he would actually accept.

But the challenge was hard to refuse: climb Mount Whitney, the tallest peak in the contiguous United States, with 90-year-old Hulda Crooks. Was she implying that he might not be able to keep up? How could he let this gutsy little great-grandmother, nearly twice his age, get away with that?

Mr. Lewis embarked on a serious conditioning program. On the day of the climb, trim, fit, and 30 pounds lighter, he made it to the 14,494-foot summit. As he stood atop Mount Whitney he sported a T-shirt that proclaimed, "By Hook or by Crooks."

> **The challenge was hard to refuse: climb Mount Whitney, the tallest peak in the contiguous United States, with 90-year-old Hulda Crooks.**

"I'm a new man," he laughed.

The congressman commented later to a news reporter, "The most challenging and exciting experience of my years in public affairs occurred as a result of joining 90-year-old Mrs. Crooks on her twenty-third ascent of Mount Whitney. The example and inspiration she provided through her commitment to good health—physical, mental, and spiritual—has contributed immensely to men and women of all ages."

Mr. Lewis continued, "The interaction between Mrs. Crooks and myself has encouraged me to take a more active role in personally promoting good health through a daily regimen of vigorous exercise, and by sponsoring health-related legislation in Washington, D.C."

Another who made it to the top that year was 11-year-old Byron Diehl. He hugged Hulda, saying, "Thank you for letting

215

me climb Mount Whitney with you."

For seven months this lad had faithfully pulled his dad out of bed for a sunrise jog "to get ready for the climb." Now, on his way down from the top, the flush of triumph eased all the pain and fatigue of those months. And the little boy's thoughts began turning to bigger dreams.

Donovan Martin, an energetic and fit 61-year-old banker from Marina Del Rey, also reached the top. "But I wouldn't have accomplished much without your inspiration," he told Hulda. "I read about you several years ago in the press, and you've been my idol ever since. If you could begin climbing Mount Whitney at age 66, well, what was wrong with my trying it at 55? That idea got me started."

And here's what a TV news correspondent had to say to Hulda after his film crew had spent four days with her on the rugged trail. "Of all the people I've met in my professional life, you are now at the top—a mighty rare person. You have given me a new perspective of life from a higher reference point. Thank you for making a difference in my life."

What is it that inspires a congressman, a young boy, a banker, and a news correspondent, along with scores of others, to climb Mount Whitney with Hulda Crooks? The climb is certainly no afternoon pleasure jaunt. In the words of reporter Steve Cooper:

> **Hulda is a teacher and a gentle conscience in the midst of a society conspicuous for its overconsumption and sedentary living.**

"Above the 12,000-foot level, although a few athletes stroll by looking superior, most folks are sweating, sucking oxygen with the force of an industrial vacuum cleaner, and feeling their legs turn to rubber. Altitude sickness can strike with its double-you-over nausea and a headache that comes on like a freight train. The sensible thing would be to hike back down to where the air is.

"But turning tail would be an excruciating embarrassment if you are walking with this incredibly strong 90-year-old vegetarian. Better to fall gasping on the trail than to admit you've been done in by cheeseburgers and pizza."

Older Can Be Better

You are the oldest known person to have reached the 14,494-foot summit of Mount Whitney reads a plaque awarded her by the U.S. Department of Agriculture. She also holds nine national records for women more than 80 years old in the quarter and half marathons, as well as in the 10-kilometer run. Her exploits have found their way into national newspapers, magazines, network television, health films, and even into the *Congressional Record.*

Even so, Hulda shuns the limelight. Continues Cooper, "She is a teacher and a gentle conscience in the midst of a society conspicuous for its overconsumption and sedentary living. She wishes to use her mountain fame only as a means to have her message heard.

"Hulda Crooks is the grandmother everyone dreams of having. Her blue eyes sparkle with fun, her laugh is infectious and disarming, and her grit is as true as her character. A spunky sense of adventure is one of her hallmarks.

"No one is around her for more than five minutes without knowing she has an active faith in God and a desire to see others healthy. Ten minutes, and you'll know she is a Seventh-day Adventist who shuns meat and advocates a life of simplicity."

On her climb in August 1986, threatening weather and washed-out trails stopped Hulda at 13,777 feet. So she settled herself on a rock and called her "class" to order. "I call this high-altitude evangelism," she said, eyes twinkling at other hikers who gathered around her. "I can share my philosophy about health and good living and faith. Rich or poor, wise or foolish, we are limited to one body per customer. No exchanges, trade-ins, or replacements. And only one lease on life is granted. The body's performance during that lease is largely dependent on the intelligent care we give to it."

Zeroing in on today's go-now-pay-later generation, she worries about their obsession with the present and their unawareness of their future health. "Research indicates that a healthful lifestyle can hold back the aging process as much as 30 years," she points out. "Thirty extra years of good health is like an extension of youth. Who could turn down a bargain like that?"

Hulda is herself a living example of her message. A recent fitness evaluation at Loma Linda University's Center for Health Promotion rated her cardiovascular level as that of a healthy 60-year-old. Hulda explains what can happen when people don't exercise.

"Muscles that are not used atrophy; bones not put under stress lose minerals and become weak; joints not moved sufficiently, as in walking, working, or other forms of exercise, become stiff from disuse."

Obviously her 90-year-old bones and joints are neither stiff nor weak. What is her secret? As if anticipating the question, she continues, "No amount of exotic foods, costly elixirs, vitamins, minerals, or other supplements will save the body from deterioration if your way of life is at fault." She then spells out her formula for a healthful lifestyle: "Learn to enjoy good food, simply prepared—whole grain breads and cereals, fresh fruits, vegetables, and legumes, eaten at regular mealtimes. Between meals, drink a quart or more of water each day. Get regular exercise. You don't have to climb mountains or run marathons, but nearly everyone can walk. In fact, recent studies rate walking ahead of nearly every other form of exercise."

But this is only part of Hulda's story. Her commitment to good health includes more than the physical. "We are also spiritual beings," she says earnestly. "The Good Book tells us to love God not only with all our strength, but with all our heart, mind, and soul. We need to count the happy moments of each day and be grateful for whatever good comes to us, be it seemingly ever so little."

> **"We need to count the happy moments of each day and be grateful for whatever good comes to us, be it seemingly ever so little."**

She visibly relaxes, and a soft glow climbs over her features. "There is too much depression, particularly among older people. Talk of things that give joy. Linger over each find with a thankful heart. This will grow into a most rewarding habit. If a person has faith in God and hope for the future, he or she can go through anything. It's adversity that makes us grow strong."

Her audience has become her extended family. Smiling now, she dispenses some grandmotherly advice. "It's never too early, and it's also never too late, to get started. Health is your prize for living in harmony with the laws established by your Creator."

An hour has passed. Hulda is rejuvenated. She looks toward

the surrounding peaks. "The mountains give you strength. Here is where you build character," she concludes.

The 50 or so listeners scarcely moved while she talked. Now they press in to hug her, to kiss her cheek, and have their picture taken with her.

"I want to be like you when I get old," a teenager says admiringly.

"It doesn't come easy," Hulda tells her. "You've got to start right now and work for it."

"Are you ever going to slow down?" another asks.

"Why? So old age can catch me?" Her wit and humor are razor-sharp.

Old age won't catch Hulda, if she can help it. An early interest in healthful living led her to adopt a vegetarian diet as a teenager, a commitment she has kept for 72 years. Always a lover of the outdoors, she has gardened, raised goats, calves, puppies, and birds, and enjoyed frequent hiking and camping trips. But it wasn't until sorrow and tragedy nearly overwhelmed her that she turned to the mountains in earnest.

Hulda keeps fit with brisk, daily walks of two to four miles. As the date approaches for a major climb, she goes to nearby foothills for further conditioning. There are 269 officially registered mountain peaks in southern California, and since age 81 she has climbed 86 of them. Hardly a week passes that she doesn't have speaking appointments in different parts of the country. And hardly a day passes that someone doesn't find her door. She still does volunteer work for the School of Health at Loma Linda University, and she is authoring a book of object lessons drawn from nature and mountain climbing.

Hulda Crooks is a legend while she lives, a woman with a message of health and faith who lives what she preaches. She says she never expected to live this long, but intends to keep living life to the fullest as long as she is able.

• • •

During their Whitney climb, Congressman Lewis challenged Hulda to climb the Capitol dome stairs later that year to promote National Women's Sports Day.

"Hulda Crooks has been known to make mountains into molehills," the Los Angeles *Times* reported after she had zipped up the 365 steps inside the Capitol's dome. "Her 90-year-old legs were still warming up when she reached the top."

"I'm not out of breath yet," she said. "I thought we were just getting started when they told me we were on the top landing."

Her trip to Washington, D.C., included a ceremony in honor of her achievements and a visit with President Reagan in the Oval Office.

● ● ●

The following year (1987), she accepted a challenge to climb Japan's highest peak, 12,388-foot high Mount Fuji. According to news reports, just minutes before daybreak, in true Japanese fashion, Hulda Crooks, the 91-year-old walking wonder from Loma Linda, triumphantly set her foot on Mount Fuji's summit. More than 20 television crews from Japanese news agencies and other international media had given her an early-morning send-off three days earlier. Now only a few media people were left to flash the accomplishment around the world: *Hulda did it again! The oldest woman to stand on Japan's sacred mountain.*

Because of her 22 record-breaking climbs of Mount Whitney, she had become known as "Grandma Whitney." But when she reached the summit of Mount Fuji, another name was bestowed. A 15-foot banner declared, "You made it, Grandma Fuji. A new record at 91."

However, the title was not earned without a struggle. Slippery volcanic rock, blustery winds, and an unrelenting up-grade almost saw Mount Fuji win out. At 2:30 a.m., just 400 feet below the summit, it was pitch dark and below freezing. It looked as though the climb might be over. Hulda was exhausted. Her parka was covered with black sand hurled at her by cutting winds. Her face an expressionless mask of black grime, she slumped onto the small folding stool.

"Look, Mrs. Crooks!" a companion squealed. "Look at the lights! You can see the top!"

Hulda stood up. Like the champion athlete she was, she tapped a deep well of determination. Her face relaxed, her body tightened, and she pushed on.

"This is like life," she said from her mountaintop pulpit. "We take a few steps forward, and then we may be blown a few steps back. The important thing is to keep your eye on the goal and move toward it—step by step."

As with all her mountain climbing, Hulda Crooks spread her message of healthful living. "The Lord gave us a very fine design for a body. If we use it properly, we can enjoy life and appreciate all of His beautiful creation. That's my message. And it's not just for old people. Take care of yourself when you are young so you have something left when you're older."

On her way down she was met by a group of U.S. marines who had climbed up to meet her.

"She is an incredible person. After talking to her, I'm swearing off Big Macs," vowed U.S. Marine officer Les Miller.

Later she met U.S. ambassador Mike Mansfield at a reception. "When it came time for tea, he did the serving," she said. "I'm having the time of my life at age 91! Who says old age starts at 65? That's when life began for me."

The very next evening on ABC's *World News Tonight,* Peter Jennings honored Hulda Crooks as "Person of the Week." For six minutes he focused on her life and her Seventh-day Adventist faith and lifestyle.

"'Grandma Whitney,' alias 'Grandma Fuji,' has not only conquered mountain peaks—she has warmed the hearts of people around the world," he concluded.

> **Because of her 22 record-breaking climbs of Mount Whitney, she had become known as "Grandma Whitney."**

Hulda Crooks climbed Mount Whitney for the last time at age 91, a month after her Fuji climb. She continued to hike lesser peaks for the next several years as her energy permitted.

Hulda lived independently in her own home well into her ninety-seventh year. On Christmas 1995 I visited her at her Linda Vista retirement apartment in Loma Linda. She looked well, and her face crinkled with pleasure when she saw me. She's still quite agile, but her fear of falling and "breaking something" has limited her excursions.

Her blue eyes still twinkled as she proudly showed me the "Charles Weniger Medal for Excellence" she'd been awarded in 1995. She worried, though. "This medal is too valuable for me to keep," she confided. "I want to donate it to the Heritage Room at the Loma Linda University Library. I realize I'm not going to live forever, and I want to be sure this is in a safe place."

• • •

Feeling Fit

In May 1996 Hulda Crooks celebrated her 100th birthday. *Gentle Mountain Tamer Turns 100,* announced the San Bernardino *Sun* in bold black letters on the front page of its Sunday news section. The article was accompanied by a picture of Hulda in full color. *In the craggy, granite neighborhood of Mount Whitney, a jagged peak bears the name of an uncommon woman who scaled lofty mountains and hiked steep canyons, refusing to age humbly,* wrote reporter M. S. Enkoji.

"This kind of honor is usually bestowed on the dead," explained Hulda Crooks, the woman for whom Crooks Peak is named. "It's usually in memory of someone. But I'm not in memory—at least not yet," she added, grinning.

However, there yet remained one unfulfilled dream in Hulda's life—the publication of her book, a collection of nature nuggets with spiritual applications. On this special day at a large reception in her honor at the Quiet Hour radiobroadcast headquarters, she was presented with her book, *Conquering Life's Mountains,* published at last. More than 600 well-wishers were present, including U.S. congressman Jerry Lewis, who read telegrams from California's governor Pete Wilson, President Bill Clinton and First Lady Hillary Rodham Clinton, and many others. More than 500 books were sold, and Hulda was busy most of this happy day autographing as many as possible.

Obviously, old age *is* beginning to catch up with her, but she wears it as a badge of pride. "I'm not waiting around for the grim reaper," she hastens to add. "I'm waiting for the Life-giver."

The incredible hiking Hulda. A mighty rare person, indeed.

Appendix 1:
The NEWSTART Lifestyle

Appendix 2:
The NEWSTART Diets

Appendix 3:
Making NEWSTART Practical

Appendix 4:
Health Resources

Feeling Fit

APPENDIX 1:
The NEWSTART Lifestyle

NEWSTART® is a registered trademark of Weimar Institute's NEWSTART Lifestyle Program and is used by permission in this book also to represent other programs using the same principles. NEWSTART is an acronym based on the eight natural remedies Ellen White writes about in the book *The Ministry of Healing:* **N**utrition, **E**xercise, **W**ater, **S**unshine, **T**emperance, **A**ir, **R**est, and **T**rust in God.

The NEWSTART lifestyle, as used in this book, represents a return to a stricter adherence to these principles than is seen in the lifestyles of most people today. The following is a brief summary of the eight basic guidelines for healthful living as adapted from *Dynamic Living,* by Aileen Ludington, M.D., and Hans Diehl, Dr.H.Sc., M.P.H., pp. 200, 201.

NUTRITION
Nourish your body with healthful, full-fiber, nutrient-rich foods.
Increasingly move toward a totally vegetarian lifestyle.
Enhance digestion by breaking the snack habit.
Schedule regular mealtimes, four to five hours apart.
Eat larger breakfasts and smaller evening meals.

EXERCISE
Strengthen your body and increase your enjoyment of life with daily active exercise, outdoors if possible.
Aim for at least 30 minutes of exercise a day. Walking is the safest exercise and one of the best.
Physical exercise reduces stress, combats depression, restores energy, improves sleep, and strengthens bones.

WATER
Rinse out and refresh your insides by drinking a glass or two of water on arising.
Come alive with an alternating hot and cold shower in the morning.
Lighten your body's metabolic load and increase circulation by drinking plenty of water—around six to eight glasses per day.

SUNSHINE

Pull back the drapes! Fill your home with sunshine! It will lift your spirits, brighten your day, and improve your health!

Spend at least a few minutes outdoors every day.

TEMPERANCE

Live a balanced life. Make time for work, play, rest, exercise, and hobbies.

Nurture relationships and spiritual growth.

Protect your body from harmful substances, such as tobacco, alcohol, caffeine, and most drugs.

AIR

Air out your house daily. Sleep in a room with good ventilation.

Keep your lungs healthy by taking frequent deep breaths. Walk outdoors when possible.

Fill your house with green plants that absorb carbon dioxide and increase the oxygen.

REST

Reserve seven to eight hours a night for rest and sleep. The body needs this time to repair and restore the damage of daily wear and tear.

Go to bed early enough to wake up feeling refreshed.

Devote time to a change of pace. Attend church, go on a picnic, plant a garden, pursue a hobby, take relaxing, enjoyable vacations.

TRUST

A life of quality and fulfillment includes spiritual growth and development.

Love, faith, trust, and hope are health-enhancing. And they bring rewards that endure.

Trust in God augments all healing—physical, mental, emotional, and spiritual.

APPENDIX 2:
The NEWSTART Diets

WHAT ARE THE **NEWSTART** DIETS?

"Grains, fruits, nuts, and vegetables constitute the diet chosen for us by our Creator. These foods, prepared in as simple and natural a manner as possible, are the most healthful and nourishing. They impart a strength, a power of endurance, and a vigor of intellect that are not afforded by a more complex and stimulating diet" *(The Ministry of Healing,* pp. 296, 297).

The above words are familiar to those who are acquainted with the Adventist lifestyle, yet few of us realize how far the foods we are eating today have veered from these principles. For practical purposes, NEWSTART diets are divided into two types:

1. The Preventive (Optimal) Diet for healthy people. This diet will prevent most of today's lifestyle diseases. Notice how it compares with the average American (Western) diet:

	Western Diet/day	Preventive Diet/day
Fats and oils	35-40%*	15-20%*
Sugar	35 tsp.	minimal
Cholesterol	500 mg.	50 mg.
Salt	15-20 gm.	5 gm.
Fiber	10 gm.	40-50 gm.

---

*percent of calories

2. The Reversal Diet is for those who already have one or more of the lifestyle diseases. We now know that a *much stricter* limitation of fat and cholesterol intake will, over time, result in a gradual unplugging of clogged arteries. Improved circulation of the blood allows affected areas to start healing and can sometimes bring about a reversal of the disease. Here is how the Reversal Diet compares to the Preventive Diet:

	Preventive Diet/day	Reversal Diet/day
Fats and Oils	15-20%*	10% or less*
Sugar	minimal	minimal
Cholesterol	50 mg.	0 mg.
Salt	5 gm.	5 gm.
Fiber	40-50 gm.	40-50 gm.

---

*percent of total calories

The NEWSTART Diets

Dr. Dean Ornish is presently the world authority on the reversal of coronary artery disease. He says, "The Reversal Diet is a very low-fat vegetarian diet that includes no animal products, except egg whites and nonfat dairy. This is what was consumed by the patients in our study whose coronary heart disease began to reverse. I am convinced that this is the world's healthiest diet for most adults, whether or not they have heart disease."

The NEWSTART Reversal Diet is the same as the one Dr. Ornish uses, except that in most cases it does not include animal products (egg whites and nonfat dairy). This is because milk and eggs are among the most common causes of food allergies. Omitting these foods often provides considerable relief for people suffering from allergic rhinitis (sniffles), asthma, rheumatoid arthritis, and other autoimmune diseases. Also, a high percentage of adults show some degree of lactose intolerance (inability to digest milk sugar properly), evidenced by bloating, excessive gas, cramps, and diarrhea.

LIFESTYLE (WESTERN) DISEASES

These are the principal diseases for which diet and lifestyle play a major role:
1. Coronary heart disease (heart attacks)
2. Cerebral vascular disease (strokes)
3. Hypertension (high blood pressure)
4. Type II (adult) diabetes
5. Certain cancers
6. Osteoporosis (brittle bones)
7. Obesity
8. Some kinds of arthritis

For more information, see Hans Diehl and Aileen Ludington, "Lifestyle Diseases," *Dynamic Living* (Hagerstown, Md.: Review and Herald Pub. Assn., 1995).

APPENDIX 3:
Making NEWSTART Practical

THE PROBLEM

To make a dent in the battle against the present epidemic of Western lifestyle diseases, we must break with the lethal excesses of today's Western diet. We need a simpler, more natural way to eat.

THE SOLUTION

There is a diet that can not only protect against these diseases but also help heal them. Such a diet consists of a wide variety of foods eaten as grown, simply prepared with sparing use of fats, oils, sugars, and salt. It contains very few refined, processed, concentrated, or engineered products. Animal foods, if used, are strictly limited. (See *Dynamic Living,* p. 197.)

HOW TO DO IT

Remember the following principles:

It isn't the occasional good deed or bad deed that determines the character: it is the thrust of the daily life.

It isn't the occasional binge or feast that jeopardizes health, but what we eat day by day.

Tastes are not inherited; they are cultivated.

Those who persevere in eating healthful food will, after a time, begin to relish it.

Those who are engaged in active, physical labor do not need to be as careful as to the quality or quantity of their food as those persons of sedentary pursuits.

When we are doing sedentary work, even plain food should be eaten sparingly.

> Habit is an intersection of:
> knowledge—what to do and why
> skill—how to do it
> desire—want to do it

What we are, basically, is a composite of our habits. We can choose our habits.

Making NEWSTART Practical

TIPS FOR SUCCESS

1. Make changes slowly, especially with children.

2. Buy at least two Crock-Pots. Use one to slow-cook cereal during the night, to be hot and ready for breakfast. In the other, slow-cook different kinds of stews, using a variety of legumes and other vegetables.

3. Find a good source of whole-grain bread. Such bread, served with stew (above), provides a healthy meal when time is limited. Freeze leftover stew for later use.

4. Make whole-wheat bread at home when you can. The good smells will help your children learn to enjoy such bread.

5. Pick up fresh fruits and vegetables once or twice a week. Ready-to-eat veggies stored in the refrigerator are attractive, as well as quick and easy to use.

6. Don't buy snacks. Offer children fresh fruit or raw veggies, arranged attractively in bite sizes on individual plates at mealtimes. Use fresh fruit on cereal instead of sugar.

7. Reserve desserts for special occasions. They will be much more appreciated.

COMMENTS

Today's dietary message is "low fat, high fiber." Most of the fat and all of the cholesterol comes from animal foods. On the other hand, unrefined plant foods are not only full of fiber and almost all other nutrients the body can possibly need, they contain protective substances against cancer (phytochemicals). Yet surveys show that Westerners eat little fruit, except for juice, and even fewer vegetables. Add sedentary lifestyle to all that, and it's no wonder people today are in trouble.

Adventists have been favored with unique and insightful knowledge of how God works through His own natural laws to keep us in health and to help heal when disease strikes. Yet because such a lifestyle doesn't easily fit today's world, many resist making needed changes.

People often ask: "How many [NEWSTART] people stick with the program? How much good does it do?"

My answer: "Those who follow the program 80 percent get 80 percent better, those who follow 50 percent get 50 percent better, and so on, down to 10 percent. I don't believe anyone leaves a NEWSTART program without being at least 10 percent better. Even 10 percent is better than nothing."

Basic Guidelines

(from *Dynamic Living,* pp. 198, 199)

EAT LESS:

Visible fats and oils. Strictly limit fatty meats, cooking and salad oils, sauces, dressings, and shortening. Use margarine and nuts very sparingly. Avoid frying. Instead, sauté with a little water in nonstick pans.

Sugars. Limit sugar, honey, molasses, syrups, pastries, candy, cookies, soft drinks, and sugar-rich desserts, such as pudding, pies, cakes, and ice cream. Save these foods for special occasions.

Foods containing cholesterol. Strictly limit meat, sausages, egg yolks, and liver. Limit dairy products, if used, to low-fat cheeses and nonfat milk products. If you eat fish and poultry, use them sparingly.

Salt. Use minimal salt during cooking. Banish the salt-shaker. Strictly limit highly salted products such as pickles, crackers, soy sauce, salted popcorn, nuts, chips, pretzels, and garlic salt.

Alcohol. Avoid alcohol in all forms, as well as caffeinated beverages such as coffee, colas, and black tea.

EAT MORE:

 Whole grains. Freely use brown rice, millet, barley, corn, wheat, and rye. Also, eat freely of whole-grain products, such as breads, pastas, shredded wheat, and tortillas.

 Tubers and legumes. Freely use all kinds of white potatoes, sweet potatoes, and yams (without high-fat toppings). Enjoy peas, lentils, chickpeas, and beans of every kind.

 Fruits and vegetables. Eat several fresh, whole fruits every day. Limit fiber-poor fruit juices and fruits canned in syrup. Eat a variety of vegetables daily. Enjoy fresh salads with low-calorie, low-salt dressings.

 Water. Drink six to eight glasses of water a day. Vary the routine with a twist of lemon and occasional herb teas.

 Hearty breakfasts. Enjoy hot multigrain cereals, fresh fruit, and whole-wheat toast. Jump-start your day.

APPENDIX 4:

Resources

The following is a *partial list* that includes those resources known to measure up to NEWSTART standards.

BOOKS, MAGAZINES, PRINTED MATERIAL:

Better Health Productions
—Resources on health: books, videos, tapes, cookbooks.
Hans Diehl
P. O. Box 1761
Loma Linda, CA 92373
909-825-1888.

Dynamic Living
—A book that tells you how to take charge of your health.
Aileen Ludington, MD and Hans Diehl, DrHSc, MPH
Review and Herald Publishing Association (1995)
55 West Oak Ridge Drive
Hagerstown, MD 21740
800-765-6955

Dynamic Living Workbook
—Study guide for above book.
Aileen Ludington and Lawson Dumbeck
Review and Herald Publishing Association (1995)
55 West Oak Ridge Drive
Hagerstown, MD 21740
800-765-6955

Energized!
—A collection of short readings by more than 165 writers, offering spiritual insights, personal testimonies, and professional expertise.
Kay Kuzma, Jan Kuzma, and DeWitt Williams, compilers
Review and Herald Publishing Association (1997)
55 West Oak Ridge Drive
Hagerstown, MD 21740
800-765-6955

Resources

Lifeline Health Letter
—Bi-monthly magazine with cutting-edge health information.
Hans Diehl and Aileen Ludington, editors
P. O. Box 1761
Loma Linda, CA 92354

The Quiet Hour's *New Way of Life*
—Radiobroadcast. (Send for free catalog of health brochures and radio logs of program.)
P. O. Box 3000
Redlands, CA 92373
909-793-2588

Listen
—Bi-monthly magazine communicating temperance principles to teens and young adults, emphasizing positive alternatives and lifestyle choices.
Lincoln Steed, editor
Review and Herald Publishing Association
55 West Oak Ridge Drive
Hagerstown, MD 21740
800-456-3991 (Monday-Thursday, 8:00 a.m.-5:00 p.m. EST)

Vibrant Life
—Bi-monthly magazine for healthful living.
Larry Becker, editor
Review and Herald Publishing Association
55 West Oak Ridge Drive
Hagerstown, MD 21740
800-456-3991 (Monday-Thursday, 8:00 a.m.-5:00 p.m. EST)

LIVE-IN EDUCATION CENTERS:

Black Hills Health and Education Center
—Seminars, publications, live-in programs.
P. O. Box 1
Hermosa, SD 57744
605-255-4101

Colonial Health and Education Center
—Live-in program for lifestyle changes, health education, food prep/cooking schools.
18750 NE Sixty-third
Harrah, OK 73045
405-454-6653

East Pasco Medical Center
—Lifestyle change programs, support groups, seminars, health screenings.
7050 Gall Boulevard
Zephyrhills, FL 33541
813-788-0411

Eden Valley Lifestyle Center
—Lifestyle programs for smoking cessation, stress management, weight control.
6263 North County Road 29
Loveland, CO 80538
800-637-9355

Lifestyle Center of America
—Live-in program for lifestyle changes, specializing in prevention/reversal of heart disease, diabetes, and hypertension; weight reduction; smoking cessation.
Route 1, Box 4001
Sulphur, OK 73086
800-213-8955

Lifestyle Medicine Institute
—"Seminars for Lifestyle Change"
Hans Diehl
P. O. Box 474
Loma Linda, CA 92373
909-796-7676

Mission Health Promotion Center
—Residential NEWSTART programs in an exotic tropical setting (6-day and 14-day)
Muaklek, Saraburi
Thailand 18180

NEWSTART Lifestyle Center
—Live-in program for lifestyle change, videos, health foods, health publications, seminars.
Weimar Institute
Weimar, CA 95730
916-637-4111

Resources

Poland Springs Health Institute
—Live-in health conditioning programs, health seminars, publications.
Route 1, P. O. Box 4300
Poland Springs, ME 04274
207-998-2795

St. Helena Hospital and Health Center
—Live-in and walk-in programs for smoking cessation, chemical addiction recovery, weight control, Brainworks Unlimited, personalized health programs.
650 Sanitarium Road
P. O. Box 250
Deer Park, CA 94576
707-963-3611

Silver Hills Guest House
—Live-in programs featuring hydrotherapy, exercise, massage, cooking lessons.
Rural Route 2
Lumby, British Columbia
Canada V0E 2G0

Uuchi Pines Health Conditioning Center
—Live-in programs, seminars, extensive health publications.
Route 1, P. O. Box 273
Seale, AL 37875
205-855-4764

Wildwood Lifestyle Center
—Live-in programs, seminars, health publications.
Wildwood Sanitarium and Hospital
Wildwood, GA 30757
404-820-1493

To Maximize Your Own Health and Lifestyle

Dynamic Living

In 52 power-packed chapters of health knowledge, *Dynamic Living* gives you the information you need to take charge of your own health and well-being. Written by Dr. Aileen Ludington and Dr. Hans Diehl, its cutting-edge scientific information is easy to understand and apply to your life. You'll gain a basic knowledge of nutritional principles; discover how to prevent and often reverse lifestyle diseases such as hypertension, coronary heart disease, and adult diabetes; lose weight without going hungry; and learn how to balance your life for optimum health—physically, mentally, emotionally, and spiritually.

Dynamic Living Workbook

Enhance your journey toward better health with this companion workbook. Step by step, through an abundance of creative exercises and activities, you will become more personally involved in the process of maximizing your health.

Book, US$10.99, Cdn$15.99.
Workbook, US$5.99, Cdn$8.49.

Feel the Difference
Vibrant Life Makes

Vibrant Life lets you know how to feel your best. Get life-changing advice on nutrition and fitness. Discover simple ways to avoid disease. Enjoy wholesome, delicious recipes.

If you want to experience more strength, more energy, and more peace of mind, subscribe to *Vibrant Life,* the one health magazine that recognizes the connection between faith in God and your well-being.

Credit card orders: 1-800-765-6955

☐ Please send me one year (six issues) of *Vibrant Life* for only US$9.97.* I save 33 percent off the cover price of US$15.00.

Your Name _____

Address _____

City _____

State, Zip _____

Please add US$5.10 per subscription for addresses outside the U.S.A. as well as GST in Canada. Mail with check or money order to: *Vibrant Life,* P.O. Box 1119, Hagerstown, MD 21741.

*Price subject to change.   651-04-0